The Creative Worship Leader's Toolbox

Tools, Tips, and Ideas for Engaging Services

Philip C. Garside

Philip
Garside
Publishing Ltd.

Paperback International edition 2025:
ISBN 9781991027948

Also available

New Zealand paperback: ISBN 9781991027931
Paperback print-on-demand USA: ISBN 9798265662941

PDF: ISBN 9781991027955
ePub / Kindle: ISBN 9781991027962

Philip Garside Publishing Ltd
39 Sydenham Street, Northland,
Wellington 6012
Aotearoa New Zealand

sales@philipgarsidebooks.com
www.philipgarsidebooks.com

Front cover image:
Created by Philip Garside.
Shows the Natural Treasures Collage idea.

Contents

Preface

Leading worship well will draw on all your skills, tools, and creative ideas. Over time, I have discovered that leading worship is both an art and a craft – a blend of spiritual sensitivity, creative imagination, and practical know-how. It is a ministry that calls you to be both deeply rooted in Scripture and attuned to the present moment, holding together tradition and freshness, depth and accessibility.

This book gathers the lessons, experiments, and inspirations I've collected through years of worship leading, writing, and resource creation. Some ideas have been sparked by unexpected conversations, a passing image, or a simple object that carried surprising symbolic weight. Others have grown out of deliberate planning, reflection, and learning.

My ideas here aren't the only way to do things – far from it. They are starting points, adaptable to different styles of worship, denominational traditions, and the unique personalities of leaders and congregations. You may find that some suggestions slot perfectly into your current practice, while others may challenge you to try something completely different. Either way, my hope is that you will treat this book as a personal toolbox – a place to rummage, select, and adapt to suit the needs of your faith community.

Worship leadership is a journey, and no two leaders will travel the same path. My invitation is simple: explore, experiment, and allow your creativity to be shaped by prayer and purpose. If this book helps you to lead services that are more engaging, more thoughtful, and more alive to the movement of the Spirit, then it will have done its job.

Accessing links to websites and other digital resources referred to in this book

I have compiled into one PDF document all the links to websites and other digital resources referred to in this book.

Throughout the book I prompt you to: (See Links PDF at end.)

A link to download the PDF is provided at the end of the book.

After downloading the PDF, click the links within it to access the resources.

Introduction

This book is designed for anyone who wants to lead worship with confidence, variety, and imagination. It is for people just starting out and for the seasoned worship leader who feels their service plans could do with a little more sparkle. If you have ever wished for a practical guide that balances solid technique with fresh inspiration, this is it.

The book is divided into three sections. The first, Skills and Techniques, is all about the craft of worship leading – from foundational abilities like planning and structuring a service, to advanced skills such as integrating multimedia, collaborating with musicians, and shaping moments of reflection. These chapters focus on how to create a flow, keep people engaged, and handle the unexpected with grace. They are about equipping you with the confidence to make intentional choices, whether you are planning months in advance or responding on the spot.

The second, Ideas for Worship, is a treasure chest of creative starting points – music, songs, objects, metaphors, and seasonal resources – adaptable to a wide range of contexts. Some are simple, single-element ideas you can drop into any service; others are more elaborate frameworks you can build an entire gathering around. Each one comes with practical notes on preparation, adaptation, and how to introduce it in a way that draws your congregation in.

The last section Prayers, Liturgy & Children's Talks contains samples of various types of prayers and starter suggestions for children's talks. This material is drawn from our weekly *Worship at Hand* resources series.

You don't need to read the book from start to finish. Instead, think of it as a collection of tools you can dip into whenever you need inspiration or practical help. Each chapter is self-contained, so you can try out a single idea or combine several to create a richer, more varied service. Some readers may work through the Skills and Techniques first to strengthen their foundations; others might dive straight into the creative ideas and let their planning evolve from there. However you choose to approach it, keep in mind that the most engaging worship happens when solid skills and thoughtful preparation meet creativity and openness to the Spirit.

Ultimately, this book is about expanding your possibilities. It is about giving you the confidence to think beyond the default options, to draw from a wide range of resources, and to offer your congregation worship that is fresh without being gimmicky, rooted without being rigid. Your voice as a worship leader matters – and this toolbox is here to help you use it well.

Skills and Techniques

Introduction to Skills and Techniques

Before we explore creative ideas for worship, it is worth pausing to strengthen the foundations on which those ideas will rest. Without solid skills and a clear understanding of your role, even the most exciting concept can fall flat. Think of this section as the framework of your worship-leading craft – principles, methods, and habits that give your creativity the best possible chance to flourish.

We begin with Foundational Skills: the essential practices that help you prepare well, lead with confidence, and create a natural flow in your services. From there, we will build towards Advanced Techniques: approaches that stretch your abilities and open up new ways of connecting with your congregation. Some of these techniques may feel familiar, others may challenge you to step outside your comfort zone – and that's a good thing.

Treat this part of the book as training for your worship muscles. The more you develop these skills, the more freedom you will have to adapt, innovate, and respond to the Spirit in the moment. Once we have laid this groundwork, we will be ready to explore the full range of creative ideas that can make worship truly come alive.

Foundational Skills

1 – What's in Your Toolbox? Part 1 – Identify your skills

This chapter encourages you to take stock of your skills – both professional and amateur – that can contribute to leading creative worship. I share my own "toolbox" of abilities, ranging from music, publishing, and public speaking to sound/video production and online marketing, highlighting the importance of acknowledging and valuing one's talents. Readers are then tasked with listing their own skills in preparation for learning how to develop new ones in the next chapter.

• • •

Introduction

This is the first of three chapters focusing on how to assess, acquire, nurture, and use your talents and skills when leading creative worship services.

In New Zealand, we often have a cultural habit of downplaying our skills. We're modest about our talents and achievements because we don't want to seem as if we're putting ourselves above others.

When it comes to leading creative worship, that attitude isn't helpful. We need to shift our mindset and acknowledge the abilities God has given us.

Below is my own "toolbox" of skills that help me as a worship leader. Some I've developed over decades; others are more recent. Some I do at a professional level, others just for fun – but all are useful.

Sound Recording

I've been recording sound since my teens, starting with transferring 45s and LPs onto cassette tapes – "mix tapes." My tools back then were analogue turntables, amplifiers, radio cassette players, and tape decks.

When home computers arrived in the early 1990s, I began recording and editing audio digitally, starting with Goldwave and now using Audacity. I also use a Tascam digital audio recorder for choir concerts and my son Chris's jazz band sessions. In addition, I can record church services directly through the sound system for later editing.

Video Recording

In the late 1980s, I was recording TV shows onto VHS tapes. Today, I can shoot video on a smart phone or digital camera, edit it on my computer, and upload it online. Recently I learned to create square promotional videos using Canva.

Singing & Playing Musical Instruments

Music runs in my family – my parents were good singers, and my mum was a piano teacher. In my late teens and early 20s, I took guitar, piano, and flute lessons. Music even played a role in bringing Heather and me together.

These days, I'm good at finger-picking guitar to accompany myself and capable of backing others. In the 1980s, I sang in our church choir, gaining fantastic training through weekly rehearsals and Sunday services. I'm an average sight-singer, but I'm loud, generally in tune, and I love singing in harmony.

Composing & Typesetting Music

I can write lyrics and melodies, adding basic guitar chords. About 20 years ago, I learned how to typeset music for our congregation's Singing Group, and I still use Noteworthy Composer for this work.

Publishing

Since publishing my first book in 1999, I've produced more than 75 titles. My process involves editing authors' manuscripts, designing and typesetting, arranging printing, creating eBooks, and listing editions for sale online. I use Adobe Photoshop and InDesign for print, and Jutoh for eBooks.

Reading

I read 70 or more books a year – mostly thrillers and spy novels, but at least 10 theological or Christian works as well.

Writing

In the 1990s, I wrote and typeset instruction manuals for Bank of New Zealand and later trained further in technical writing. This taught me to write clearly and logically so readers can understand information easily.

Public Speaking

I joined Drama Christi in 1979, moving from non-speaking roles to speaking and even leading roles as my confidence grew. This experience helped me become comfortable speaking in front of people – though I still get a few nerves.

Websites, Facebook & Online Marketing

I built my first website in 1997, learning through books and experimentation. Since then, I've explored Facebook and other marketing tools to promote books, recordings, and concerts. Recently, I created an e-commerce site for my business and have been learning more about email marketing and interpreting customer data.

People Better Than Me

For every skill I've listed, I know someone who's better. I'm the second-best sound and video editor in my family, the third-equal best musician, and the second-best singer. Heather outshines me in harmonising songs and setting guitar chords.

In publishing, Roger Steele – my mentor – will always have the edge. And when it comes to online marketing, I'm learning from *The Social Sales Girls*, a Canadian and US-based coaching group whose coaches have far more expertise than me.

• • •

Your Homework

Make your own list – on paper or computer – of the skills and talents you have that could be useful for leading creative worship. Think broadly, just as you would in a brainstorming session.

In the next chapter, we'll look at how to learn new skills.

2 – What's in Your Toolbox? Part 2 – Learning New Skills

This chapter focuses on the importance of lifelong learning for worship leaders, exploring how to acquire new theological, technical, and creative skills. I share personal experiences with learning through books, podcasts, YouTube, online news, eBooks, audio books, and digital tools, as well as practical tips for self-directed study. Readers are encouraged to reflect on their preferred learning methods and experiment with new ones in preparation for integrating all their skills in the final part of the series.

• • •

Introduction

This is the second of three chapters about assessing, acquiring, nurturing, and using your talents and skills when leading worship services.

In education circles, there's a popular mantra: be a lifelong learner. I'm living proof that learning doesn't stop after school – I'm 65, and most of what I've learned has happened since I left formal education at 17.

During my Lay Preacher training, I took Old and New Testament papers by correspondence through EIDTS (Ecumenical Institute for Distance Theological Studies). I passed, but I'll admit – I'm not a great student. I have huge respect for those who thrive in that setting.

So, where and how do I learn new theology, skills, and ideas today?

Books

Books are miraculous. An author writes their story or ideas, and years – or even centuries – later, we get to "sit down" with them in conversation. As worship leaders, all books, even fiction – mysteries and thrillers included – broaden our empathy by helping us see the world through someone else's eyes.

My theological reading has taken me on a 30-year journey. I began with one question: Did the miracles in the Bible really happen? After a few false starts, I discovered writers whose views resonated: John Dominic Crossan, John Spong, Bart Ehrman, Diana Butler Bass, Marcus Borg, Richard Rohr, and Brian McLaren. These voices helped shape my identity as a progressive Christian.

I've also learned that changing one's theology is rarely quick or easy. Respect for others' perspectives is vital – no matter how brilliant we think our latest sermon was, we can't expect instant agreement. And we should always remember there's more than one way to interpret the Bible, and we could be wrong.

Podcasts

Podcasts – free, downloadable audio interviews and presentations – are a favourite learning tool for me. I listen while walking to the shops or doing the dishes.

For years, I enjoyed John Shuck's *Progressive Spirit* podcast, often borrowing or buying books by authors he interviewed. While that podcast has ended, there's a list of similar Progressive Christianity podcasts on Feedspot (see Links PDF at end).

I also recommend the BBC History Extra podcast, (see Links PDF at end) which often covers church history and theology. One fascinating episode featured Irving Finkel discussing a Babylonian clay tablet from around 1850 BC with a flood story like Noah's Ark, which fuelled a sermon on how Jewish exiles in Babylon writing down Old Testament stories for the first time were influenced by local myths.

Another excellent source of thoughtful podcasts about contemporary ministry is the Lewis Centre for Church Leadership (see Links PDF at end).

YouTube Videos

We've ditched broadcast TV and now watch YouTube and other documentaries on our TV via a computer. This freedom from scheduled programming gives us access to a vast range of content – on our terms.

Online News Sources

I keep *The Guardian* UK, Radio NZ, Google News, and Flipboard apps on my smart phone, browsing regularly for stories that spark ideas or help me track social trends.

Audio books & eBooks

I borrow audio books from the public library, listening to them just like podcasts. On my Kindle, I've amassed over 400 eBooks. They're cheaper than print, take up no shelf space, and make note-taking easy. Highlighted quotes and notes become a goldmine, when I think, "What did Crossan say about this?" months later.

Learning New Technical & Multimedia Skills

I've been using computers since the late 1980s. The are vital for both worship preparation and my publishing business. When I started with computers, learning how to use software meant wading through the thick printed manuals that came in the box with the disks. Now, I search Google or YouTube for tutorials – nearly always finding exactly what I need for InDesign, Photoshop, Word, or Excel.

AI Tools

In the last year, I've been exploring AI tools like ChatGPT and Google's Notebook LM (see chapters 13 and 14).

• • •

Your Homework

Reflect on these questions:

- How do I learn new ideas, skills, or techniques?
- Which methods work best for me?
- What new learning approach will I try next?

In the third and final chapter of What's in Your Toolbox, we'll explore how to bring all your skills together to serve your church and local community.

3 – What's in Your Toolbox? Part 3 – Putting it all together

This chapter brings together the skills, experiences, and learning from the previous two chapters, showing how they integrate into a meaningful ministry of worship leading, service, and community involvement. I show how my unique blend of talents supports preaching, music, design, technical work, and leadership – while also emphasizing the importance of balance, saying no to overcommitment, and giving back freely. Readers are challenged to identify their own unique "toolbox" of abilities to serve their congregation and local community.

• • •

Introduction

This is the third chapter about assessing, acquiring, nurturing, and using your talents and skills to lead creative worship – and to support other aspects of ministry.

Using My Skills in Worship

Preaching and leading worship call on almost everything in my skill set. My goal is to create services where prayers, music, children's time, and sermons work together as a coherent whole.

My decades of choral singing experience help me choose hymns – both traditional and new – that fit the service's theme. My theological reading informs my sermons, offering the congregation fresh perspectives on the day's Bible readings. Drama Christi experience helps me overcome my nervousness when leading a service.

Facebook, Posters & Programmes

Since October 2020, I've been posting service details on our congregation's Facebook page: designing banner images, live-streaming services, and sharing audio recordings afterward. These posts help publicize our church and allow members who can't attend to worship from home.

I also enjoy designing posters, flyers, and programme booklets for Festival Singers and Drama Christi.

Commitments I Keep

I have two fixed weekly commitments:

- Sunday mornings at church – I arrive 30 minutes before the start (45 minutes if I'm leading), to help set up and run the service.
- Monday evenings at Festival Singers – 7:00 rehearsals in Newlands.

These are non-negotiable. I make them because smooth-running services matter – technical glitches can distract from both worship and the preacher's message.

Giving Back

I don't charge for the work I do for the church, Festival Singers (where I'm secretary), or Drama Christi. These groups have given me so much:

- The church provides a faith community.
- Festival Singers lets me learn and perform beautiful music.
- Drama Christi shaped me as a young adult – and now our son Alexander plays a leading role in the group.

Through my publishing business, I produce and sell resources – especially worship materials – that help ministers, worship leaders, and congregations. I also distribute the New Zealand Hymnbook Trust's music in print, digital, and recorded formats.

Integrating Life & Work

At 65, I've found a fulfilling balance between my work, family, church, and choir involvements – a personal "ministry" of service to others. These parts of my life feed each other: music from Festival Singers makes its way into the Singing Group and sometimes into worship; book research for my publishing business sparks sermon ideas; and new theological insights flow back into the congregation.

The Power of Saying No

Maintaining balance means having the confidence to say no to requests that would stretch me too thin. A little pressure now and then is fine – but getting burnt out through ongoing stress and overcommitment helps no one.

I've declined administrative roles for the Lower North Island Synod and turned down offers to lead services at other churches, even when there was payment involved. My priority is serving my own congregation, especially during times when we've been without a minister.

What's in YOUR Toolbox?

Plenty of people I know are better at each individual skill I use. But no one else has my exact combination of abilities, creative energy, and experiences – and the same is true for you.

If you've been reading this series thinking, "I can't do what Philip does," you're right – you can't. And that's the point. The question isn't what I can do – it's: What's in YOUR toolbox?

What skills and talents do you have – or want to learn – that you can use to serve your congregation, church, and local community?

4 – Constructing a Service 1 – The Elements of a Service

This chapter outlines the key elements of the church services I lead, offering a detailed, step-by-step framework for structuring worship in a way that is engaging, balanced, and thematically coherent. I explain the purpose and flow of each component – from welcome and prayers to readings, music, community sharing, and closing – along with practical tips on timing, content, and congregation participation. Readers are encouraged to reflect on their own service structures, challenges, and possible improvements.

• • •

This is the first in a seven-chapter series on Constructing a Service. In this series, I'll share how I structure a typical service and create the content for it.

In this chapter, we'll focus on The Elements of a Service.

Upcoming chapters will cover:

- Choosing Hymns, Songs & Waiata
- Finding or Writing Prayers and Liturgy
- Writing Your Sermon
- Introducing the Theme / Story Time / Children's Talk
- Designing & Typesetting the Order of Service
- Two sample services I've led

Introduction

Planning a church service can be both time-consuming and complex. Having a clear structure makes the process smoother, more efficient, and more meaningful for both the leader and the congregation.

This chapter outlines the essential components I use in the services I lead, with practical notes on where to place hymns, prayers, liturgy, and the sermon. Whether you are an experienced minister or a new lay worship leader seeking a reliable framework, you can adapt this structure to a variety of worship settings.

I see the service as having four main sections:

- **Opening** – Welcome to Prayer of Approach & Words of Assurance
- **Exploring the Theme** – Theme introduction to hymn after the Sermon
- **Community Time** – Sharing the Peace to Offering & Blessing of the Offering
- **Closing** – Closing Hymn to The Grace

Sections in the Services I Lead

Welcome & Introduction
Welcome everyone – both those present in person and those joining online if the service is being live-streamed. Mention which Sunday of the church year it is (e.g. the third Sunday in Lent) and briefly highlight the Bible readings and the theme for the service.

Call to Worship
A short responsive prayer of 6–8 stanzas. You can also use hymn lyrics, poetry, or a paraphrase of the Psalm for the day.

Lighting the Candle(s)
A short litany said together as the candle is lit. (I prefer to leave the candle burning until after the service – for me, snuffing it out at the end feels like extinguishing the light.)

Opening Prayer
A brief prayer led by the worship leader, often introducing the themes of the day.

Opening Hymn
A familiar hymn of praise with a singable tune.

Prayer of Approach & Words of Assurance
A responsive prayer that may acknowledge what we have failed to do, or things we have done but shouldn't have, followed by an affirmation of God's love and forgiveness.

Introducing the Theme / Children's Talk
An interactive activity for children and adults that explores the theme – such as acting out the Bible reading and discussing it briefly. Avoid just lining up children at the front asking them questions.

Hymn, Song or Waiata
An opportunity to introduce a new song that relates to the theme.

Readings
Include the full text in the printed Order of Service (without verse numbers) and break long passages into smaller paragraphs for readability. Showing the full text of the readings and prayers in the Order of Service makes the liturgy accessible to both newcomers and regular attenders.

Sermon
Delivered immediately after the readings so they are fresh in people's minds. Include images or music where appropriate.

Hymn, Song or Waiata
Choose something that reinforces the sermon's theme – either congregational or performed by a singing group.

Community Time

- **Sharing the Peace:** Invite everyone to greet each other with words such as, "God's peace be with you." This is a warm, light-hearted time that may take a while to wrap up – and that's fine!

- **Notices:** A congregation member gives updates on meetings, events, and other news. I place notices here rather than at the beginning, so latecomers don't miss them.

- **Sharing Joys, Gratitude, Sorrows & Concerns:** Invite the congregation to share things they wish to celebrate or concerns they'd like included in prayer. If nothing is shared publicly, invite people to bring to mind the things on their hearts privately as they join in the intercessions.

- **Prayers of Intercession:** Responsive prayers covering local, global, and personal needs. I include the congregational response in the printed Order of Service (e.g. Leader: "Loving God, in your mercy…" Congregation: **"Hear our prayer"**) and rehearse it with the congregation before beginning.

- **Lord's Prayer:** Show the full text in the Order of Service – whether a traditional or more modern form. I often lead it in te reo Māori, speaking at a pace that is comfortable for everyone.

- **Offering & Blessing of the Offering:** Invite the collection of monetary offerings along with food donations for the local food bank. After these are brought forward, the congregation stands to say a short, printed blessing, usually linking to the day's theme.

Closing Hymn

A familiar, uplifting hymn that ties in with the theme. This is not the time to introduce new music.

Blessing

A short paragraph, printed in the Order of Service, reflecting the service's themes. The leader stands at the front with open arms to give the blessing.

The Grace

Spoken together. I generally use the te reo Māori version.

Notes on Service Length & Preparation

With a 10-minute sermon, the above structure usually results in a 60-minute service (+/– 5 minutes).

I am not comfortable praying or speaking entirely off the cuff, so I write down everything I will say, including the sermon and liturgy.

I prepare two versions of the Order of Service:

- Congregation version – shorter, with hymns and responsive text.
- Leader's version – longer, with full text of everything I will say.

• • •

Questions for Reflection

- How do you currently structure your worship services?
- What challenges do you face in planning a service, and how do you overcome them?
- If you could change one aspect of your church's service structure, what would it be and why?

5 – Constructing a Service 2 – Choosing Hymns, Songs & Waiata

This chapter offers a practical guide for worship leaders on selecting hymns, songs, and waiata that fit a service's theme, engage the congregation, and balance tradition with fresh material. It covers sources for finding music, working with musicians, handling textual variations and inclusive language, choosing singable tunes, and placing hymns effectively within the service. I also provide tips on teaching new songs, and ensuring music is both meaningful and accessible to the congregation.

• • •

Introduction

Worship leaders – do you sometimes find it difficult to choose hymns, songs, and waiata that not only fit your service theme but are also singable, meaningful, and engaging for your congregation? Do you wonder how to strike a balance between traditional and new material, how to handle inclusive language, or how to collaborate effectively with musicians?

This chapter offers suggestions for selecting hymns and songs that enhance congregational participation, deepen the service's message, and create an uplifting worship experience. We'll also look at working well with organists, introducing new material, and approaching inclusive language carefully and thoughtfully.

The Purpose of Hymns, Songs & Waiata in Worship

In this chapter, I'm focusing on music sung by the congregation during the service – not items performed solely by a choir, singing group, or band.

Wellington composer and church musician Jonathan Berkahn puts it beautifully in the introduction to Festival Singers' CD *People of the Light*:

> "…church is one of the few places left where ordinary people – people who don't consider themselves musicians – are still expected to sing, as a matter of course. And just as cooking is far too important to be left to professional chefs, I believe singing is far too important to be left to singers. Secondly, church is a place where people, also as a matter of course, wrestle with and reflect upon deep things: life and death, good and evil, justice and mercy. To enter church is to join a conversation

that has been going on about these things for a few thousand years now."

Singing in worship isn't only about praising God – it's also a way to explore the deeper aspects of faith. Hymns often use simpler, more direct language than sermons or liturgy, giving people an accessible way to engage with the service's themes.

The physical act of singing together connects us emotionally and spiritually. A rousing hymn can unite and uplift a congregation, while memorable melodies help the words stay with us throughout the week.

Sources for Hymns, Songs & Waiata

Start with what you already have. Begin by looking through the hymnbooks and songbooks your congregation uses. Borrow copies and note hymns or songs that fit your theme or that are well-loved and familiar.

In our congregation, we often sing from the UK Methodist *Hymns and Psalms* (late 1980s) and the earlier *With One Voice*, which has a useful supplement of New Zealand hymns at the back.

The New Zealand Hymnbook Trust

The Trust has produced four collections rich with Aotearoa hymns covering many topics:

- *Alleluia Aotearoa*
- *Faith Forever Singing*
- *Carol Our Christmas*
- *Hope is Our Song*

These are well worth exploring – you can order them from us.

Talk to your organist early

A week or so before your service, discuss your theme with your organist. They may suggest hymns or tunes that fit well and are familiar to the congregation.

Local composers

Heather and I sing in Festival Singers, where we've performed many new works by Jonathan Berkahn, the choir's accompanist. Several are suitable for congregational use, and we've successfully introduced them in our church.

Write your own
If you compose hymns or songs, why not teach one to your congregation? It's rewarding for both you and them.

CDs, YouTube & other recordings
Great for finding new material – but remember, you'll need to source or create lyrics, arrange the tune for your setting, and be ready to accompany it yourself. If you give them enough time, your organist or other church musicians may be able to help you with this.

Textual Variations

If you're using a hymnbook in the pews, there's no problem. But when projecting lyrics or printing them in an Order of Service, you'll often find variations in wording.

Tips:
- Hymnary.org is a great online resource, but their "Representative Text" may differ from your congregation's usual version.
- Always read through and sing the text to ensure it fits the tune.
- If you adapt the wording, mark it clearly after the title, e.g. "(adapted)."

Inclusive Language

Where possible, I adjust gendered terms to be more inclusive:

"Good Christian men, rejoice" becomes "Good Christians all, rejoice"

"Close-binding all mankind" becomes "Close-binding humankind"

Sometimes a full rewrite is needed:

"Brother, let me be your servant" becomes "Brother, sister, let me serve you"

References to God as male – such as "Father," "He," or "Him" – are harder to change effectively. I usually leave these unless a natural, meaningful alternative fits the rhythm and sense of the hymn.

Choosing Tunes

It's easy to assume your preferred tune for a hymn is everyone else's, but that's not always the case. If the accompanist plays a different tune, follow their lead and keep the singing going – don't stop the service.

As a courtesy, I email the organist my hymn list (with tunes) by Wednesday night. This gives them time to suggest a more familiar or better-suited tune.

If you're introducing a new one, ask them to play a full verse and refrain before the congregation joins in.

Words or Tune – which is more important?

If a hymn text fits your theme perfectly but the tune is awkward or uninspiring, first check for another tune with the same metre. If you can't find one, it's better to drop the hymn than risk discouraging the congregation with a melody they can't sing well.

Placement of Hymns in the Service

- Opening & Closing – Use rousing, familiar hymns with strong tunes, even if the language is a little dated.

- Middle – Ideal for introducing new songs once the congregation is warmed up.

Further Considerations

Think about vocal ability. Avoid tunes that are too high, too low, or contain difficult intervals – unless you know your congregation can handle them.

Balance the familiar with the new. Include enough well-known hymns to make people feel comfortable, and introduce new material gradually, repeating it over several weeks.

Incorporate waiata thoughtfully. Introduce waiata respectfully, provide translations, and explain the meaning to deepen understanding. For more on this, see chapter 29.

Check licensing and copyright. Ensure your church has the right licences (e.g. from CCLI – Christian Copyright Licensing International) before reproducing or performing newer songs.

• • •

Over to You

- What challenges do you face when choosing hymns, songs, or waiata for your services?

- Who can you collaborate with to help with music in your services?

6 – Constructing a Service 3 – Finding or Writing Prayers and Liturgy

This chapter explains the purpose and flow of different types of prayers and liturgical elements in a worship service, from the Call to Worship to the Benediction and The Grace. It offers a wide range of resources for finding or creating prayers, including books, subscriptions, and the use of AI tools, along with practical tips for writing in a natural, theologically consistent voice. The emphasis is on intentional preparation, understanding the role of each element, and using language that engages the congregation while staying true to the leader's own theology and style.

• • •

Introduction

As a worship leader, crafting meaningful prayers and liturgy for your services can be both rewarding and daunting. Week after week, you need to find words that are theologically sound, spiritually engaging, and relevant to your congregation.

If you've ever wondered where to begin, how to structure your prayers, or how to make them truly resonate, this chapter is for you. Here you'll discover clear, practical advice for selecting or writing prayers and liturgical elements that flow naturally through a worship service. We'll look at the purpose behind each part of the liturgy, explore helpful resources, and also see how tools like AI can support your creativity.

Purpose of Prayers and Other Liturgy

Each type of prayer I include in services has its own purpose and distinctive characteristics.

Call to Worship

Purpose: Gathers and centres the congregation for worship, inviting them into a shared sacred space and setting the tone for the service.

- Invites communal participation and focus on God.
- Acknowledges God's presence and calls for attentive worship.
- Often poetic, rhythmic, and inclusive in language.
- Usually leader calls and congregation responds.

Lighting the Candle/s

Purpose: Symbolises Christ's light in the world and focuses prayers on specific themes, e.g. healing, justice, remembrance.

- Symbolic act using light as a representation of Christ or hope.
- Thematically tailored.
- Invites reflective prayer.
- Usually said together.

Opening Prayer

Purpose: Invokes God's presence and dedicates the worship time to God, offering praise and thanksgiving.

- Includes praise and adoration.
- Acknowledges God's role in creation and life.
- Requests God's presence and guidance.
- Usually said by the leader, but can be call and response.

Prayer of Approach

Purpose: Acknowledges human frailty and dependence on God, inviting God's presence and offering ourselves in worship.

- Themes of humility and repentance.
- Opens hearts to God's presence.
- Prepares the congregation spiritually.
- Usually call and response.

Words of Assurance

Purpose: Affirms God's love for us after the prayer of approach.

- Offers reassurance, comfort, and renewal.
- Often based on scripture or tradition.
- Usually said by the leader.

Prayers of Intercession

Purpose: Offers prayers for the needs of the world, the community, and individuals.

- Includes global, local, and personal concerns.
- Uses a call and response structure (bidding and response).
- Often thematic, focusing on justice, healing, and peace.

Lord's Prayer

Purpose: A communal recitation of the prayer Jesus taught, expressing shared faith and dependence on God.

- Universal and ecumenical.
- Profound in its simplicity and theology.
- Always spoken or sung together.
- Can use a traditional or more modern form
- If sung in English, we use the setting at #676 in *With One Voice*.
- When spoken, I generally use the te reo Māori version.

Offertory Prayer (Blessing of the Offering)

Purpose: Dedicates offerings of money, time, and talent to God's service.

- Expresses gratitude for God's provision.
- Affirms commitment to ministry and mission.
- Also mention offerings given via online banking or automatic payments.
- Usually said together.

Benediction

Purpose: Sends the congregation out with God's blessing and a sense of mission.

- Pronounces peace and blessing.
- Encourages discipleship and service.
- Sometimes refers to the Trinity.
- Said by the leader.

The Grace

Purpose: A traditional closing blessing invoking God's grace, love, and fellowship.

- Scriptural and Trinitarian in form.
- Shared aloud by all present as we bless each other.
- I generally now use the te reo Māori version.

Sources

These liturgy resources are available on subscription:

- *Worship at Hand* – Ready-to-use worship service scripts that equip leaders with theologically rich liturgies rooted in the Revised Common Lectionary
- *Gathering* – Worship planning tools for every Sunday, with prayers, sermon starters, and hymn suggestions.

Excellent books for prayers and liturgy include:

- *Prayers for Southern People* – Responsive prayers and liturgies for the Southern Hemisphere.
- *Prayers for Southern Seasons* – Prayers and poems for the church year in Aotearoa New Zealand.
- *Lay Preaching Basics* – Tools and resources for lay preachers and worship leaders (eBook).
- *Joyful Spirit Bubbling* – Poems, prayers, and reflections for the seasons of faith in New Zealand.

Writing Prayers

Why not try writing your own? Start small – with a Call to Worship or Opening Prayer.

You can see an example of mine, *God is in the small things*, in chapter 36.

AI tools like ChatGPT can also be a fun way to get started. Generate a draft, then adapt it so it reflects your voice and theology. For tips on doing this well, see chapter 12.

Top Tips

Once you've drafted your Order of Service, print it and read everything aloud – this reveals awkward phrases and helps you prepare to lead.

I always write out the full text of prayers and liturgy in my Order of Service.

I don't pray off the cuff; it's not my strength.

Prayers can be conversational, formal, or informal (but never casual). Keep the language simple and every day.

Allow a small pause for silence between elements of the service. Keep things moving, but don't rush.

Conclusion

Leading worship isn't about filling time with words – it's about crafting a sacred experience that draws people into genuine connection with God and one another.

When you understand the purpose of each prayer, choose your language thoughtfully, and prepare thoroughly, you can offer worship that's both accessible and profound. Whether you draw from published resources, write your own prayers, or use AI as a creative companion, the key is to stay true to your voice and theology.

The prayers you choose shape the congregation's worship experience. With these tools and approaches, you can prepare something thoughtful, inspiring, and uniquely yours.

7 – Constructing a Service 4 – Writing Your Sermon

This chapter provides three practical methods for writing sermons – traditional study and drafting, a hybrid approach using dictation and AI, and fully AI-generated drafts – each designed to help worship leaders create meaningful, engaging messages. It outlines step-by-step processes for working with lectionary readings, developing personal insights, incorporating anecdotes, and ensuring the Good News is central. The chapter also offers guidance on editing, polishing, and rehearsing sermons to deliver them with clarity, confidence, and impact.

· · ·

Introduction

Crafting a sermon can be one of the most rewarding – and time-consuming – parts of leading worship. Whether you're a seasoned preacher or preparing your very first message, having a clear process helps you create sermons that are meaningful, memorable, and rooted in the lectionary.

In this chapter, you'll discover both traditional and tech-savvy approaches, learn how to integrate AI tools like ChatGPT into your workflow, and gain practical advice for structuring, editing, and delivering your sermon with confidence.

The Purpose of a Sermon

At its heart, a sermon is an opportunity to explore one or two Bible readings and help the congregation discover in them fresh meaning for life today. It is often the high point of the service – a moment to offer new insights, challenge assumptions, and leave people inspired. A good sermon is engaging, thought-provoking, and memorable.

Three Sermon-Writing Methods

I use the New Zealand Methodist Church's version of the Revised Common Lectionary to select readings.

Here are three approaches I've found effective.

1. Traditional Approach

- *Step 1: Gather the Bible Readings*

Go to Bible Gateway online.

- Search for each of the Lectionary readings.
- Select your preferred translation from the dropdown (top right).
- Click the settings cog above the text and untick: Cross-references, Footnotes, Verse Numbers, and Red Letter – leaving only Headings. This produces clean text.
- Copy and paste each reading into a Word document.

I like to use two contrasting translations:

- New Revised Standard Version Updated Edition – reliable and scholarly.
- The Message – vivid and conversational.

Do this for all four Lectionary readings.

- *Step 2: Annotate and Reflect*

Print your document and sit somewhere quiet.

Using a pen:

- Underline key words
- Circle phrases
- Jot down margin notes, and
- Draw arrows to connect ideas.

This free-flowing approach helps you notice which texts and translations resonate with you most.

After working through all eight readings (four texts × two versions), choose the one or two you'll preach on – usually the Gospel plus one other.

Write further notes by hand – both bullet points and sentences. I find handwriting unlocks creativity in ways typing doesn't.

- *Step 3: Write a First Draft*

Start typing your sermon. Don't self-edit. Just get your ideas down. Often a key phrase or theme will emerge to anchor your message.

- *Step 4: Fact-Check*

Verify details you're unsure of, e.g.

- How long did it take to journey by donkey from Nazareth to Bethlehem in Jesus' time?
- When did Moses live?

- *Step 5: Consult Commentaries (Later)*

Only now turn to biblical commentaries. You've already explored your own thoughts – now broaden your perspective. Commentaries are helpful, but your congregation wants to hear your ideas and voice.

- *Step 6: Add a Personal Anecdote*

Adding a brief personal story linked to your theme creates warmth and relatability.

- *Step 7: Share the Good News*

Always affirm God's love and offer hope. Ask yourself:

- What's the Good News here?
- How will I leave people encouraged?

2. Hybrid Approach – Dictation + AI

- *Dictate Your Thoughts*

Follow steps 1 and 2 above to choose your readings and annotate them. But instead of writing detailed notes, speak your thoughts into a document. As you speak, your words will be added into the document on the screen.

You can use the voice dictation tools built into Microsoft Word or Google Docs. Use the microphone that comes built into your laptop, the microphone in a separate web cam or a separate external microphone.

Speak freely and don't worry about grammar or structure. Once you run out of steam, stop. Then lightly edit for capitals and full stops, but nothing more.

- *Use ChatGPT to Organise Your Thoughts*

Paste your dictated text into ChatGPT with this prompt: .

> "Please provide a 1000-word summary of the following text. Please organise and extend the ideas."

ChatGPT will turn your raw thoughts into structured paragraphs with improved grammar, ready to shape into a sermon.

3. Ask ChatGPT to Write Your Sermon

If you're stuck, or just want a new take on the readings, let ChatGPT draft something for you.

Try prompts like:

> "Based on [Bible reading 1] and [Bible reading 2] and taking into account these key ideas: [bullet points], write a 2000-word sermon using engaging, simple, inclusive language."

Or:

> "Based on [Bible reading 1] and [Bible reading 2], write a 2000-word sermon using engaging, simple, inclusive language."

Here's a real example I used recently:

> "Please provide a 2000-word sermon based on the readings: Psalm 63:1-8 and Luke 13:1-9. Make links between the readings. Make links to the church seasons of Lent and Easter. Treat the Bible texts symbolically rather than literally. Explore the relevance of the texts to contemporary life in New Zealand in 2025. Use simple language and vivid imagery. Offer uplifting and encouraging words."

ChatGPT can generate a full sermon with a title and section headings. You can use this as a foundation and add your own voice, anecdotes, and insights.

Editing and Polishing Your Sermon

Once you have a draft – whichever way you created it – print it out and read it aloud.

Mark changes by hand:

- Fix sentences that don't make sense
- Break up long sentences
- Replace weak words with stronger ones

Type your edits and save the updated document. I often run my near-final version through ChatGPT using this prompt:

"Please edit the draft sermon text I will give you in a moment to simplify it while retaining the key content, extend the ideas in the sermon, and correct any grammar issues."

You can choose how much of the output to use – but I've found ChatGPT's suggestions are usually excellent. This version often becomes my final sermon.

On the Friday or Saturday before preaching, print your sermon and rehearse it aloud one last time. You may spot a final tweak or two, and you'll step into the pulpit more prepared and confident.

Summary

This chapter has shown you three flexible sermon-writing methods – from traditional pen-and-paper study to dictation and AI-enhanced drafting.

You've seen how to make the most of Bible translations, the lectionary, and your own reflections. You've learned when and how to bring in commentaries, where anecdotes add impact, and how to polish your final sermon for clarity and inspiration.

Whichever method you choose, the goal is the same: to speak Good News into people's lives with clarity, heart, and hope.

8 – Constructing a Service 5
– Introducing the Theme / Children's Talk

This chapter explores how the "Introducing the Theme / Children's Talk" section of a service uses creativity, interaction, and symbolism to capture attention and deepen engagement with the message. It offers practical strategies such as visual aids, active participation, symbolic actions, music, and real-life connections, along with detailed planning tips to make this segment meaningful and memorable. The emphasis is on simplicity, preparation, and leading from memory so that the activity feels natural, engaging, and spiritually enriching for all ages.

• • •

Introduction

The "Introducing the Theme / Children's Talk" part of a church service is where creativity and faith meet. It's your opportunity to capture your congregation's imagination, spark curiosity, and open the door to deeper engagement with God's message. Whether you're speaking to children, adults, or a mix of both, this section can become a highlight that sets the tone for everything that follows.

Over the years, I've experimented with many ways to make this moment both meaningful and memorable. Here are practical, proven strategies to help you bring this part of your service to life.

1. Make It Visual and Tactile

People of all ages respond to what they can see and touch. Props and visual aids grab attention, make abstract ideas concrete, and help messages stick.

- Use creative materials such as stones, leaves, or shells that participants can arrange, build, or contribute to collectively. (See chapter 16.)

- Incorporate symbolic objects like candles or water bowls to create tangible connections to spiritual themes.

- Show progression visually, e.g. arranging Beatles LPs from earliest to last to symbolise the unfolding story of the Bible.

2. Encourage Active Participation

Interactive activities transform listeners into participants, allowing them to embody the theme.

- Invite children or adults to build or arrange objects as part of a narrative, connecting their actions to the message.
- Re-enact Bible stories with people taking roles, helping everyone experience the story from within.
- Use movement-based activities, such as a procession with a net to illustrate Jesus' call to gather people.

3. Use Symbolic Actions

Rituals and gestures speak directly to the heart.

- Invite participants to make a personal sign of faith, such as dipping a finger in water and making the sign of the cross.
- Provide tangible symbols, like ringing a bell as a sign of commitment or renewal.
- Set up prayer stations where people can reflect quietly through sensory experiences.

4. Connect the Story to Everyday Life

Help people bridge the gap between ancient Scripture and today's world.

- Share modern stories of faith and resilience that echo biblical themes.
- Highlight how biblical values – like inclusivity, justice, compassion, and community – relate to current issues.

5. Encourage Reflection and Sharing

Invite participants to process and share their insights.

- Create small group discussions to reflect on the theme.
- Encourage creative responses, such as collages or arranging natural objects.
- Ask open-ended questions that spark deeper thought.

6. Use Music and Song

Music reinforces themes and creates unity.

- Teach a simple song or refrain connected to the theme, repeating it at key moments.

- Use music as a response, linking it to prayers or reflections. (See chapter 30.)

7. Practical Steps for Planning

To make this section smooth and impactful:

- Identify Your Theme – Be clear on the Scripture or message you want to highlight.

- Choose Your Approach – Decide on props, storytelling, role-play, symbolic actions, or a mix.

- Gather Materials – Prepare visual aids in advance.

- Brief Your Helpers – Ensure anyone assisting understands their role; rehearse briefly if needed.

- Reflect and Connect – After the activity, link what was experienced back to the service theme.

Top Tip – Lead from Memory

To be most effective, lead this part of the service without reading from notes. This makes it feel spontaneous and invites participation. I write my plan, quickly scan it before starting, then speak freely – keeping to the main points rather than memorising word-for-word.

If you can't deliver it from memory, the activity is probably too complex. Simplify it to one or two actions with a clear takeaway message.

Conclusion

This part of the service is a precious space where theology meets creativity, and words give way to experience. It can engage minds, touch hearts, and create memories that last well beyond Sunday.

Experiment with the ideas here – try new props, invite participation in new ways, and share your successes with others.

Keep your focus on making the theme of the day come alive in ways that are meaningful, memorable, and spiritually enriching. When you do, you'll see how powerfully this moment can draw people deeper into worship.

(See also Chapter 52 for several ideas for this slot.)

9 – Constructing a Service 6
– Design & Typeset the Order of Service

This chapter explains how to design and typeset an Order of Service in Microsoft Word, so it is clear, professional, and easy for the congregation to follow. It provides step-by-step guidance on A5 booklet formatting, font and spacing choices, laying out prayers and hymns for readability, avoiding bad line breaks, and preparing a final PDF for printing. Practical tips also cover troubleshooting formatting issues, printing with Adobe Reader, and organising service materials files on your computer for efficient preparation.

• • •

Introduction

This chapter will help you:

- Understand why good design matters for an Order of Service and how it enhances the flow of worship

- Learn how to use Microsoft Word effectively to design an order of service without needing expensive or complex design software

- Get clear, step-by-step instructions for formatting A5 booklets, including margins, fonts, and spacing

- Discover how to format prayers, hymns, and liturgies to improve readability and congregational participation

- Learn practical ways to avoid bad line breaks that disrupt flow and clarity in both print and slides

- Save time with smart formatting tips like using Find & Replace and paragraph spacing short cuts

- Gain confidence in preparing professional-looking Orders of Service that are easy to read and print

- Learn how to print your booklet using Adobe Reader's booklet settings, whether your printer is duplex (can print on two sides) or not

- Pick up tips on organising service materials files efficiently on your computer, ready for use on Sunday

- Access a real-life sample to inspire your own formatting choices.

A well-designed Order of Service document helps the service to flow smoothly. A poorly laid-out Order of Service can distract people from the worship and make it harder for them to engage.

I use Microsoft Word to create my Orders of Service. It's simpler than using more sophisticated and complex design software like Publisher or InDesign, and Word gives me all the control I need for this task.

Here are some practical tips for good design.

Use Word for Design and Save the Document as a PDF for Printing

I'm assuming that your Order of Service will be printed on two sides of A4 sheets and folded to make an A5 booklet.

Step-by-step:

1. In Word (or your preferred word processing software), create an A5 document: in the top menu go: File | New | Layout | Size | A5

2. Set margins to 1cm on all four sides:
    Go: Layout | Margins | Custom Margins, then set Top, Left, Bottom and Right margins to 1cm

3. Set page orientation to Portrait

4. When finished, save your Word document as usual, then save a copy as a PDF:
    Go: File | Save As, and in the dropdown where it says Word Document (*.docx), click the down arrow and choose PDF (*.pdf), then click Save.

PDF files are easier to print as booklets – see *Printing Your PDF Booklet* at the end of this chapter.

Formatting Your Text

- Use one font only throughout the document – e.g. Calibri – and stick to one colour: black.
- Use font size, bold and italics to differentiate headings, body text, credits etc., rather than different fonts.
- Set all body text – hymns, prayers, and liturgy – to the same size, e.g. 11pt.

These factors unify the design and make the document easier to read.

(See Links PDF at end to view the PDF of my 23 March 2025 Order of Service for examples of the design tips I outline below.)

Cover Page

Aim for a clean, uncluttered layout with plenty of white space. Centre the text and image on the page.

At our church, we typically show the following on the cover:

- Church logo
- Church name and street address
- Website address
- Date and which Sunday it is in the church year
- Welcome in te reo Māori and English
- An image that reflects the theme of the service. (See chapter 11 about creating worship images using AI)
- Title of the service theme
- The congregation's vision statement
- A short statement about the nature of our church
- Greetings in the languages of our four congregations and in te reo.

Page 2 and Onwards

Start with these details centred at the top of page 2:

- Order of Service
- Congregation name
- Date and which Sunday in the church year
- Names of the leader(s), organist, and any other featured musicians

The rest of the service text then follows using the structure I outlined in chapter 4.

Formatting tips

- Make section headings bold and align them with the left-hand margin
- Insert a hard line break (ENTER) before each heading to create white space between sections
- **Indent** the body text of each section one level to the right: select the text and press CTRL+M (To undo the indent: press CTRL+SHIFT+M)

Formatting Prayers and Liturgy

For responsive prayers, use plain text for the leader's parts and **bold** for the congregation's responses.

Avoid formatting it like this:

> Leader: text
> People: text

That takes up too much space and isn't as clear.

- Use a soft line break (SHIFT+ENTER) after the leader's text to begin the congregation's response on the next line
- Use a hard line break (ENTER) at the end of each response to split stanzas into paragraphs

To control paragraph spacing for the whole document:

1. Select all the text
2. Go: Home | Paragraph | Options icon (bottom-right corner)
3. In the Spacing section, set:
   - Before: 0 pt
   - After: 4 pt (or 6 pt for more generous spacing)
   - Line Spacing: Single
   - Untick "Don't add space between paragraphs of the same style"

Click OK.

Show or hide hidden characters

It helps to display paragraph marks (¶) and line break symbols (↵) while formatting text.

- Go: Home | Paragraph section | ¶ symbol
  or press CTRL+SHIFT+* to toggle display of hidden characters on or off

This lets you clearly see soft line breaks (↵) and paragraph breaks (¶) – which is especially helpful for formatting responsive prayers and hymns.

In some cases (e.g. Words of Assurance, Lord's Prayer, Blessing of the Offering), you may want to indent the text one more step for visual clarity. Select the text and press CTRL+M.

Formatting Hymns

Each line within a verse should end with a soft line break (SHIFT+ENTER). Only the final line of each verse or refrain should use a paragraph break (ENTER).

If copying hymn text from a source like Hymnary.org:

1. Paste the text into Word
2. Select all the hymn text and reset it to **Normal style**: (CTRL+SHIFT+N)
3. Delete any existing verse numbers

Turn on hidden characters with CTRL+SHIFT+*. You'll probably see a paragraph mark (¶) at the end of each line.

You can:

- Manually replace each paragraph mark with a soft line break (SHIFT+ENTER), or
- Use Find and Replace to do it quickly:
  - Select the hymn text
  - Press CTRL+H
  - In "Find what", type: ^p (lowercase p)
  - In "Replace with", type: ^l (lowercase L)
  - Do you want to search the rest of the document? Click No.

This will reformat the hymn into a continuous paragraph.

Then, at the end of each verse, select the soft line break and press ENTER to insert a paragraph break.

Now:

- Set paragraph spacing to 4 points
- Indent the whole hymn one level: CTRL+M
- Indent each refrain one additional level: CTRL+M again

Add verse numbers:

1. Select the whole hymn text
2. Go Home | Paragraph | and click the Numbering icon (1. 2. 3.)
3. To remove numbering from a refrain, select just the refrain text and click the numbering icon again

4. If numbering starts at a number other than 1:

- Click the dropdown next to the numbering icon
- Choose Set Numbering Value
- Tick Start new list and set value to 1

If you're short on space and want to reduce the number of pages in your document, you can try setting the hymn in a two-column table. For example, see the final hymn *Jesu, lover of my soul* in the 23 March 2025 service sample.

Steps:

1. Go: Insert | Table and Choose the number of columns and rows
2. Paste each verse into a separate cell
3. Make cells borders invisible in the printed document:
   - Select all cells
   - Go: Table Design | Borders | No Border

Formatting hymn text in table cells can be fiddly – give yourself time to adjust the layout, numbering and spacing.

Avoid Bad Line Breaks

Here's an example of a poorly laid out hymn verse. The bad line breaks and the fact that the hymn and tune (while attractive) were new to us, meant that the singing did not go well in the service. It wasn't clear where the lines ended and hence where to take a breath.

Poor version:

> We are the young, our lives are a mystery; we
> are the old, who yearn for your face; we have
> been sung throughout all of history, called to
> be light to the whole human race.
> Gather us in, the lost and the forsaken; gather
> us in, the proud and the strong; give us a
> heart so meek and so lowly, give us the
> courage to enter the song.

Improved version:

> We are the young, our lives are a mystery;
> we are the old, who yearn for your face;
> we have been sung throughout all of history,
> called to be light to the whole human race.

Gather us in, the lost and the forsaken;
gather us in, the proud and the strong;
give us a heart so meek and so lowly,
give us the courage to enter the song.

Use the same principle for prayers: read the text aloud and insert line breaks where it feels natural to pause or breathe – usually at commas or full stops.

Apply the same care to hymn texts in PowerPoint slides. I use 36pt black text on a white background. Don't reduce the text size to squeeze a whole verse on to one slide – split the text across two slides instead.

Credits

Where I include credits for hymns and Bible translations within the service text, I make these much smaller, e.g. 8 or 9pt.

At the end of the Order of Service, I include:

- Details of prayer and liturgy books, and other published materials used
- Image titles and sources
- Websites referenced
- Our church's CCLI licence information

Formatting Not Working?

If text formatting is behaving unpredictably, try this:

1. Select all text
2. Reset to Normal style: CTRL+SHIFT+N
   This will left-align everything and revert to the default font (e.g. Times New Roman)
   Bold, italics, and line breaks will be retained
3. Then:
   - Choose your preferred font (e.g. Calibri) and size (e.g. 11 pt)
   - Reset paragraph spacing to 4 pt
   - Re-apply indents and numbering as needed for prayers, hymns, and liturgies

If you are struggling to get text in various places to fit on one line, try selecting all the text and choosing a half step smaller text size for the whole document, e.g. reducing from 11 points to 10.5 points. Don't go any smaller than this as it will be too hard to read.

Printing Your PDF Booklet

If you haven't already, install Adobe Reader software, which is free.

To print:

1. Open your PDF in Adobe Reader
2. Go File | Print
3. In the dialogue box, set:
   - Pages to Print: All
   - Page Size & Handling: Booklet
   - Booklet Subset: Both sides
   - Binding: Left
   - Orientation: Portrait
   - Tick Auto-rotate pages within each sheet
4. Click Print.

If you have a duplex printer, it will print both sides automatically.

If your printer is single-sided, follow the on-screen instructions to re-feed the pages manually.

Once printed, collate and fold the A4 sheets to create your A5 booklet. Proofread carefully and make final edits in Word and re-save the document as a PDF, before printing copies for the congregation.

Having completed my PDFs, I then email them to our church office who print the Orders of Service and email copies to the congregation.

Top Tip

I create a separate folder for each service I lead, called,
e.g. Wesley 2025-03-23 PG

Into this folder I save all related files – Word documents, PDFs, PowerPoints, images, sheet music, video and sound clips. On Sunday, I copy the entire folder to a USB stick and take it to church, ready to plug into the laptop for projecting slides and playing media.

Summary

A well-designed Order of Service helps the congregation stay focused and supports the rhythm of the worship experience. Using Microsoft Word, you can create professional, readable, and attractive service sheets without needing specialised graphic design software.

By applying these principles, your Orders of Service will be easier to prepare, look more professional, and support a more seamless, meaningful worship experience.

10 – Constructing a Service 7
– Two sample services led by Philip

This final chapter presents two full sample services as practical demonstrations of the planning principles from the Constructing a Service series. Each example includes downloadable service materials, illustrates the integration of interactive activities, music, visual elements, and AI-generated liturgy, and reflects on what worked well and what could be improved. Together, they show how careful preparation, creative use of resources, and theological focus can combine to create engaging, meaningful worship experiences.

• • •

Introduction

In this last chapter in the Constructing a Service series, I offer two of my services as working examples of how to apply the principles outlined in the previous six chapters. These examples are intended to be practical, transparent, with usable ideas that you can adapt for your own context.

I hope this chapter will help you to:

- See how AI tools like ChatGPT can support sermon writing and liturgy creation
- Get inspired by fresh, context-sensitive ideas for introducing the theme visually or interactively
- Learn from my comments on what worked well and what didn't in actual services
- Access downloadable materials to adapt for your own worship setting
- Evaluate the impact of theological themes and visual storytelling in designing services.

For each of the services, I provide links to download, view or listen to:

- The Congregation's version of the Order of Service
- My Leader's version of the Order of Service, which includes notes to myself and the full text of the sermon (I use larger text and print this version to lead from)

- A Facebook live-stream video of the whole service (lower resolution to keep download file sizes down)
- An MP3 audio file of the readings and sermon
- An MP3 audio file of the entire service

For both services, I used ChatGPT to generate the prayers and liturgy (except for the te reo Lord's Prayer and The Grace) and to help shape and polish the sermon.

I encourage you to consider critically whether this AI-generated liturgy is valid and effective. In my experience, it is – and the congregation accepted and participated in the prayers and liturgy as they normally would.

> Note: I don't read aloud the bold subheadings that ChatGPT includes in the sermon text, but I do find them helpful for reminding me of the flow and context of each section while I'm presenting the sermon.

Service One: Sunday 12 January 2025 – Epiphany 1

Bible Readings: Luke 3:15-17, 21-22; Acts 8:14-17
Theme: Preparing the Way – Two Paths

I knew that I wanted to share with the congregation the poem "John, the Baptist" by Clive Sansom, from *The Witnesses and Other Poems*, which I have performed in the past with Drama Christi, the drama group based at our church. The poem offers another perspective on John and helps us to imagine what it was like to be there when Jesus was approaching. I treated the poem as another scripture reading.

There is a real sense in the Gospels that it was important to show John the Baptiser as being less important than Jesus and I wanted to discuss this in the sermon.

John's and Jesus' missions were related but different and I also discussed this in the sermon. I extended this idea into the theme that we have two different paths to choose from at the start of a new year.

To introduce the theme, we attempted a water relay activity. Six adults and children participated. Although it ran longer than expected and lost a bit of momentum, it still managed to create a physical, visual moment that reinforced the idea of the Spirit helping us work together.

Musically, the waiata *Wairua Tapu*, which the congregation had learned the previous year, was a perfect fit.

I generated the cover image using ChatGPT.

See Links PDF at end for:

- Congregation's Order of Service - PDF
- Leader's Order of Service - PDF
- Facebook Live-stream Video - Whole service
- MP3 Audio – Readings and Sermon
- MP3 Audio – Full Service
- Sheet Music for *Wairua Tapu* - PDF

Service Two: Sunday 23 March 2025 – Lent 3

Bible Readings: Psalm 63; Luke 13:1-9
Theme: Thirsting for Life: Growing Good Fruit in Dry Times

This service focused on spiritual thirst and resilience during dry seasons.

I performed my original song *Psalm 63*, arranged for two guitar parts with Heather. (Guitarists: I dropped my bottom E string to D for a deeper tone, which meant using non-standard fingering. Heather played with a capo on fret 7, with alternative chords, for a lighter texture.) I did fluff the intro and had to restart, but that's real life!

We also included a lovely setting of *There's a Wideness in God's Mercy* by local composer Jonathan Berkahn. To help the congregation sing confidently, I asked the organist to play through the refrain and first verse before we joined in.

For the Introducing the Theme section, I used two simple but effective activities: a bowl of water and a bell. Everyone came forward and took part. These were two of ten options generated by ChatGPT. They worked well as parallel experiences and were easy to set up.

I adjusted my usual Order of Service sequence so that the readings came before the Introducing the Theme activity and second hymn, which made better narrative sense for this service.

I found it challenging to link the Psalm and Gospel readings, but prompting ChatGPT for connections helped.

I also brought in a personal touch: I held up two large tomatoes I had grown in my deck garden and used them as a symbol of fruitfulness in tough times. People enjoyed this visual element.

See Links PDF at end for:

- Congregation's Order of Service - PDF
- Leader's Order of Service - PDF
- Facebook Live-stream Video - Whole service
- MP3 Audio – Readings and Sermon
- MP3 Audio – Full Service
- Sheet Music for *Psalm 63* - PDF

Conclusion

These two services show how the planning principles discussed in this series come to life in practice.

From interactive activities and contextual sermon illustrations to thoughtful liturgy and music choices, each element contributes to a rich worship experience.

We also saw how AI tools can be allies in creativity and preparation, without replacing our voice or discernment.

These examples remind us that worship is both art and offering – something we shape with care, and through which God continues to speak.

Advanced Techniques

11 – Creating an Image to use in Worship with ChatGPT AI

This chapter demonstrates how to create an historically accurate, emotionally engaging worship image using ChatGPT's AI image generation tools. Through an iterative process – starting with a simple prompt and refining details like setting, clothing, audience size, emotional tone, and cultural accuracy – I produced a final image for Luke 4:14-21 that conveyed drama and authenticity. The chapter also shares tips for crafting effective prompts, working within AI limitations, and using the finished image in the Order of Service, social media, and slide shows.

• • •

Introduction

Visual images can enhance worship by deepening engagement with Scripture.

Creating an effective image is an iterative (step-by-step) process of refining prompts to align with the biblical context and emotional impact.

Here's how I created an image using ChatGPT to illustrate Luke 4:14-21 in a service.

If you don't already have an account at ChatGPT, you can sign up for free. (See Links PDF at end.)

Step-by-Step Image Creation for Luke 4:14-21

Start with a Basic Prompt
I began with:

> "Please generate an image that illustrates the reading from Luke 4:14-21."

Which generated this image:

The result was a good start but had issues: the synagogue was too large, the crowd too big, and some clothing was too modern.

Refining for Authenticity

I adjusted the prompt:

> "Please generate an image showing Jesus talking in the synagogue in Nazareth from Luke 4:14-21. Make the building rustic and rural. Make people's clothes simple and realistic for 2000 years ago, e.g. no suit and tie. Zoom in on Jesus and show no more than 15 people listening and reacting to him. Include women in his audience."

The new image was more realistic but lacked emotional impact.

Enhancing Emotion

To capture the congregation's attention, I refined further:

> "Zoom in more on Jesus. Show fewer people in the audience. Show some of the audience being surprised by what Jesus is saying."

Nearly there! My remaining concern was that Jesus looked like a modern European.

Cultural Accuracy

I made a final request:

> "Generate an alternative image showing Jesus with a darker complexion and more Middle Eastern features."

I was delighted with this final image. The framing is tight on Jesus, and the audience is giving him their rapt attention. There is real drama in the scene.

Using the Image in Worship

- Order of Service: Printed on the booklet cover.

- Social media: Used in a Facebook post advertising the service.

- Presentation Slides: Displayed on the first slide before the service. Could also have displayed the image while the scripture was read or during the sermon.

Key Tips for AI Image Creation

- Be specific in your prompts: Detail setting, historical accuracy, audience size, and emotional tone.

- Iterate and refine: Small adjustments lead to significant improvements.

- Plan around AI limitations: When I generated these images in early 2025, free versions of ChatGPT limited image generation to three per day. If you hit such a limit before you are satisfied with the image, return to the Chat the next day and enter your requests for improving the image.

By refining AI-generated images, worship leaders can create unique, tailored visuals that enhance Scripture engagement and deepen the worship experience.

12 – Using ChatGPT AI to Craft Prayers and Liturgy

This chapter describes how I used ChatGPT to create prayers and liturgy for worship, refining broad prompts based on all four lectionary readings down to a focused selection from Acts and Luke which better matched the service themes. It highlights the benefits of AI – such as efficiency, thematic focus, adaptability, and creative variety – while also addressing potential drawbacks, including loss of pastoral nuance, theological shallowness, authorship concerns, and the risk of over-reliance. Examples of AI-generated prayers are provided, along with the author's reflections on balancing innovation with tradition so that AI enhances, rather than replaces, the personal and pastoral nature of worship leadership.

• • •

Introduction

As a Methodist Lay Preacher with 18 years of experience, I've always been passionate about preparing worship services that speak deeply to our faith community.

Here's how I explored using artificial intelligence (AI) to generate prayers and liturgy for a service with ChatGPT.

I share how I started with broad prompts based on all four lectionary readings and gradually refined my focus to just the readings from Acts and Luke.

I provide examples of the AI-assisted liturgy I used in the service and explore the advantages, challenges, and ethical questions that arise when using AI to prepare worship materials.

Refining the Focus: Acts and Luke

I began by prompting the AI with all four lectionary readings: passages from Isaiah, Psalms, Acts, and Luke.

However, I soon realised that while the insights were rich, the prayers and liturgy derived from using all four readings felt unfocused. They combined a variety of themes that, while important, didn't mesh well.

To create more focused liturgy, I refined my prompts to concentrate exclusively on Acts 8:14-17 and Luke 3:15-17, 21-22. These passages share a powerful narrative: John the Baptist's passionate call to repentance and the transformative, affirming moment of Jesus' baptism when the Holy Spirit descends.

This shift allowed the AI to generate texts that were more cohesive and relevant for the service's key themes – renewal, empowerment, and a fresh start for the new year.

One refined prompt I used was:

> "Based on Acts 8:14-17 and Luke 3:15-17, 21-22, write a responsive Call to Worship of 12 lines. Use *The Message Bible* translations of the texts."

The resulting Call to Worship was vivid and engaging:

Call to Worship

The Spirit of God is here, moving among us.
We come, ready to receive, ready to be renewed.

John the Baptiser proclaimed,
"The One who comes will ignite the Kingdom life within you!"
We gather, longing for the refining fire of God's love.

The heavens opened, and a voice declared,
"You are my beloved, chosen and marked by my love."
We stand in awe, embraced by the Creator's affirmation.

The apostles laid hands on the people,
and the Spirit filled them with new life.
We come, eager for the Spirit's power to renew and transform us.

God calls us by name, beloved and cherished,
to walk this journey of faith.
We respond with open hearts, ready to follow and worship.

Let us celebrate the Spirit's presence in us and among us!
With joy and thanksgiving, we lift our praise to God! Amen.

This output captured the essence of the scriptures – an urgent call for renewal and the comforting affirmation of God's presence – making it especially suitable for our service as we looked forward to 2025.

Advantages of Using AI in Worship

My journey with AI revealed several key benefits:

1. Efficiency and Creativity

AI generates multiple drafts and variations in moments, freeing up valuable time. This allows worship leaders to explore diverse expressions of faith and refine them quickly – like having a brainstorming partner who's always ready with new ideas.

2. Focused Thematic Output

By narrowing my prompts, the themes of the prayers were more consistent. Concentrating on the transformative messages of Acts and Luke enabled the AI to produce liturgy that got to the heart of the service – celebrating the empowerment of the Holy Spirit.

3. Diverse Expression

The AI provided several different prayer formats when prompted, which I used throughout the service:

- Call to Worship
- Candle Lighting Liturgy
- Opening Prayer
- Prayer of Approach and Words of Assurance
- Offertory Prayer
- Intercessory Prayers
- Sending Forth/Benediction

4. Adaptability

Whether you prefer traditional language or contemporary phrasing, AI-generated texts can be tailored to your theological and cultural context. For example, I specified that the prayers should use inclusive language and avoid referring to God as male.

Disadvantages and Ethical Considerations

Despite the benefits, there are important challenges and ethical concerns to keep in mind:

1. Loss of Pastoral Nuance

AI-generated prayers might lack the personal, pastoral touch that comes from years of ministry experience. Prayers reflect lived experiences of faith, and there is a risk that AI-generated texts might seem impersonal or generic. Reviewing and adapting the prayers is essential to ensuring they reflect your unique voice.

2. Theological Depth

While AI can analyse vast amounts of data, it might not fully capture deep theological insights gained through study and reflection. Carefully vetting AI-generated prayers ensures they uphold our values and convey meaningful theology.

3. Transparency and Authorship

Using AI raises questions about authorship and authenticity. How do congregations perceive prayers that are AI-assisted? In the credits at the end of the Order of Service, I included:

> "Material for this service was created by Philip Garside with the assistance of ChatGPT."

This transparency acknowledges AI as a tool, not a replacement for human insight and inspiration.

4. Dependency Risks

Over-reliance on AI could reduce creativity and pastoral sensitivity. AI should complement, not replace, traditional methods of prayerful worship preparation.

Real-World Examples from the Service

Here are a couple more specific examples:

Offertory Prayer

Prompt:

> "Based on Acts 8:14-17, write a short Offertory Prayer acknowledging God's gifts and our act of giving."

Output:

> Generous God, You pour out Your Spirit upon us,
> filling our lives with grace and abundance.
> As we offer these gifts, we do so with grateful hearts,
> acknowledging all that You have given us.
> Bless this offering, that it may bring Your love
> and hope to those in need.
> Use us and all we bring to further Your work in the world,
> through the power of Your Spirit. Amen.

Sending Forth Benediction

Prompt:

> "Based on Acts 8:14-17 and Luke 3:15-17, 21-22, create a 6-line non-responsive Benediction inspired by these texts, emphasizing God's presence and our mission."

Output:

> Go now, filled with the Spirit of God,
> who strengthens and renews you.
> Carry the light of Christ into the world,
> sharing love and hope with all.
> Walk in confidence, for you are called,
> beloved, and chosen by God.
> Let your words and actions
> reflect the grace you have received.
> May the Spirit guide your steps
> and empower your mission each day.
> Go in peace to love and serve,
> for God is with you always. Amen.

Final Thoughts: Balancing Innovation and Tradition

The AI-assisted liturgy engaged the congregation as usual, with no noticeable difference in participation.

By balancing innovation and tradition, we can use AI responsibly to enhance creativity while preserving the deep, personal connection of worship.

Why not try using some AI-generated prayers in your next service?

13 – Using AI to Help Write a Sermon

This chapter describes how I used ChatGPT to expand and refine a sermon based on 1 Samuel 1:4-20 and Mark 13:1-8, resulting in a more focused, engaging, and thematically rich message.

• • •

Introduction

I used the ChatGPT AI to improve the sermon I delivered at Wesley Methodist Church, Taranaki Street, Wellington on 17 November 2024.

I was pleased with the result and felt that the messages in the sermon were appropriate and well received.

Try this process for yourself when writing your next sermon.

Summary of the Process

1. I wrote a solid first draft of a sermon of 1077 words based on the Revised Common Lectionary readings from 1 Samuel 1:4-20 and Mark 13:1-8. I chose Eugene Peterson's *The Message* translation.

2. I submitted the draft text to ChatGPT asking it to rewrite and extend the ideas into a sermon with 2000 words. (See Links PDF at end.)

   Here's my prompt to ChatGPT:

   "In a moment I will give you the text of a draft sermon based on 1 Samuel 1:4-20 and Mark 13:1-8. Please rewrite and extend these ideas and draft a sermon with 2000 words."

3. I made minor edits to the sermon text that ChatGPT output, added back in a couple of sentences in my own words from my original draft, and delivered the resulting sermon – now 1640 words.

Comments

As I hoped, ChatGPT provided some new/extended ideas/text, shown in bold:

"For his followers, this prophecy was radical and disturbing, **a call to let go of reliance on outward forms and institutions** and turn instead toward a deeper faith rooted in God."

"While these words can seem ominous, they're also words of reassurance. **Just as labour pains signal the arrival of new life, these tribulations hint at a coming transformation.**"

"This isn't hope that naively overlooks real pain and struggle. It's **a deeper hope that can look unflinchingly at hardship** and see beyond it."

"**Nothing has changed externally**; she still has no child. **But her faith has transformed her.** She leaves the temple with an unexplainable peace, renewed by the hope that God hears her and cares for her."

"Her son Samuel grows up to be instrumental in the rise of King David, **a leader whose lineage would lead to Jesus.**"

"May we all, as individuals and as a community, take up this challenge to look forward with hope, **trusting that God is making arrangements even now, arrangements that might surprise, challenge, and ultimately bless us.**"

ChatGPT provided sub-headings throughout the sermon. I left them in the printout I preached from – as visual breaks and context reminders – but did not speak the sub-headings.

ChatGPT also improved the flow of my text, simplifying it and omitting some less relevant points.

The final sermon text

Here is the final text of the sermon I presented, based on the output from ChatGPT:

Sermon: Looking Forward with Hope

"Nation will fight nation and ruler fight ruler, over and over. Earthquakes will occur in various places. There will be famines. But these things are nothing compared to what's coming."

Let's pray:

May the words of my mouth and the meditations of all our hearts and minds be acceptable to you, O God, our strength and our hope-giver.

I have titled this sermon *Looking Forward with Hope*. Together, we'll explore how we can keep looking forward, beyond the challenges of the present, toward a future we face with trust in God's enduring promises.

The Little Apocalypse in Mark's Gospel

Our reading from Mark 13 places us at a crossroads of history, when turmoil and transformation loom large. The writer of Mark composed his gospel shortly after the destruction of the Temple in Jerusalem by the Romans, in the year 70 AD. This period, marked by the Jewish revolt against Roman rule from 66-70 AD, saw devastating violence, loss, and change. The destruction of Jerusalem and its sacred Temple upended Jewish life, shifting religious observance away from the Temple toward local synagogues, and placing increased emphasis on scripture and community-based worship.

In Mark 13, often called the "Little Apocalypse", Jesus forewarns about hardship to come. Apocalypse here doesn't simply mean "end of the world" but rather an unveiling, a revelation. As with the big Revelation of John of Patmos written 30-40 years later, that ends the New Testament, the threat is from Rome.

Here, Jesus isn't just speaking about the physical destruction of the Temple; he's revealing a deeper truth: that no institution, no structure, even the most sacred, is guaranteed to last forever.

For the disciples, this prophecy was radical and disturbing, a call to let go of reliance on outward forms and institutions and turn instead toward a deeper faith rooted in God.

As we hear Jesus' words, we might ask ourselves, how would we react if someone predicted that our church building would be torn down soon? It's not hard to imagine the shock, the sadness, the sense of instability we'd feel. And yet, Jesus speaks of such events without panic. He challenges his followers not to fixate on the physical and visible, the "stones" of our tradition, but to prepare inwardly, remaining alert, calm, and full of hope.

Enduring Relevance: Today's Struggles

Jesus' message in Mark 13 echoes with unsettling relevance today. Just as the Jewish people then faced wars, suffering, and displacement, we live in times where geopolitical conflicts, natural disasters, and economic instability can seem relentless. Ukraine and Russia are locked in a painful conflict. Israel is embroiled in ongoing tension in Gaza, Lebanon and with Iran. In every corner of the world, divisions deepen, and suffering persists.

Jesus warns, "Earthquakes will occur in various places. There will be famines. But these things are nothing compared to what's coming." While these words can seem ominous, they're also words of reassurance. Just as labour pains signal the arrival of new life, these tribulations hint at a coming transformation. Jesus calls us to hold steady, to "keep calm and carry on," and most importantly, to keep our hope anchored in God's love and faithfulness.

Our natural instinct is to ask, "When will this end?" The disciples, too, wanted a timeline, a concrete sign of the "end." But Jesus doesn't give them what they're looking for. Instead, he encourages a different focus, reminding them that faith isn't about having certainty in all circumstances; it's about trusting in God's unchanging presence amid uncertainty.

Fear or Hope?

This brings us to a fundamental question: do we look forward with fear or with hope?

Jesus teaches that while our circumstances might feel frightening, hope lies in the resilience of faith, the assurance that God is with us no matter what. This isn't hope that naively overlooks real pain and struggle. It's a deeper hope that can look unflinchingly at hardship and see beyond it.

Part 2: Hannah's Story of Hope and Transformation

Turning now to the story of Hannah in 1 Samuel, we see another powerful example of hope in the face of despair. Hannah's story is deeply moving, a story of a woman who endures significant pain, both from her inability to bear children and the taunting she faces from Elkanah's other wife, Peninnah. Each year as she made her pilgrimage to the temple, Hannah was painfully reminded of her lack of children and of society's judgment on her because of this.

Despite her anguish, Hannah persists in seeking God. She goes to the temple not to express anger but to pray for relief from her distress, laying her desires and heartbreak fully before God. Eli, the priest, initially misjudges her, thinking she's drunk, a reminder to us of how easy it is to overlook or misunderstand others' pain. Once Eli listens, he recognises her deep sincerity and blesses her. His words to her – "Go in peace. And may the God of Israel give you what you have asked of him" – offer a balm to her soul, and she leaves with renewed hope.

What happens next is remarkable. Scripture tells us that after this encounter, Hannah "ate heartily, her face radiant." Nothing has changed externally; she still has no child. But her faith has transformed her. She leaves the temple with an unexplainable peace, renewed by the hope that God hears her and cares for her. Her outward circumstances are unchanged, yet she is changed. This shift within her, this choice to leave with hope, exemplifies faith in God's timing and goodness.

God's Faithfulness and Hannah's Promise

Eventually, God answers Hannah's prayers, and she bears a son, Samuel, who will become one of Israel's greatest prophets.

Yet even in her joy, Hannah doesn't forget her promise to God. She dedicates Samuel to the Lord's service, showing that her hope was not merely self-centred but born of a true desire to live in covenant with God. Hannah's gratitude led her to an extraordinary act of faith: giving back what she'd most desired. Her son Samuel grows up to be instrumental in the rise of King David, a leader whose lineage would lead to Jesus.

Hannah's story reminds us that God's response to our prayers often comes in surprising ways and that our role is not merely to receive blessings but to respond faithfully when God grants us our heart's desires.

I love the phrase that Eugene Petersen uses in his translation "and God began making the necessary arrangements in response to what she had asked." Any child is a miraculous gift from God, and no less gracious a gift because we have asked for it.

Just as Hannah made a promise to give her son to God, we're invited to consider what we're willing to offer back to God when our prayers are answered.

Part 3: Hope for Transformation in the Church

This brings us to the life of our church today. This week our parish hosted the Methodist Conference. This was a big deal for our parish. Conference is a big deal for Te Hahi Weteriana nationally. It appoints the leaders and sets the tone and priorities for the church for the coming years. The message from this Conference is both clear and challenging: our calling is not only to change but to transform. We're called to look forward with a hopeful vision that trusts in God's plans, even when we don't have all the answers.

As a congregation, we're approaching a season of new ministry. From 2025 our parish will have three ministers, supporting four congregations in a fresh, collaborative way. This is a change, and change is rarely comfortable. The truth is, we don't have a blueprint for exactly how this new structure will work. But, like Hannah, we can choose to trust and hope, knowing that God is guiding us forward.

The way the combined choir met, worked together in four rehearsals, and performed so well on the Saturday afternoon of Conference has given me renewed confidence for Wesley's future.

This collaboration, this unity in purpose, reflects the kind of spirit we need in our parish as we move into the future. The choir's success shows that when we bring our diverse talents together with a shared purpose, we can create something worthwhile.

A Call to Radical Hope and Faith

So, how do we look forward with hope?

We don't have to ignore the difficulties or uncertainties we face. We can acknowledge them and even grieve the loss of what's familiar. But in the midst of these realities, we're called to cultivate a faith like Hannah's, a faith that trusts God with both our sorrow and our joy, and a faith that offers our blessings back to God in service.

In Mark's gospel, Jesus warns of difficult times but urges his followers not to let fear consume them. He speaks of birth pains, signalling that something new and good is on the way. Our hope lies in believing that God is working through us, birthing new life, and we are participants in this divine transformation.

As a church, we have good reason to look forward with hope. We're part of a faith community that cares, encourages, and uplifts. And just as Hannah found new strength in her encounter with Eli, we find strength and peace in coming together to worship, to support one another, and to serve God.

May we, like Hannah, approach God with our whole hearts, laying down our burdens and acknowledging our blessings. And may we, like Jesus, face the uncertainties of the future with courage, hope, and unwavering trust in God's promises.

In Closing

As individuals and as a community, let's take up the challenge to look forward with hope, trusting that God is making arrangements even now, arrangements that will surprise, stretch, and ultimately bless us. Amen.

14 – Revelations About Your Preaching from Notebook LM

This chapter explores how I used Google's free AI tool, Notebook LM, to create an audio interview based on the text of my book of collected sermons. The AI-generated voices accurately summarised my theology, highlighted recurring themes, and offered affirming feedback, helping me reflect on my preaching style and strengths. Other preachers could use Notebook LM to assess their theology, gain encouragement, identify areas for growth, and spark ideas for future sermons.

• • •

Introduction

Are you curious about how AI can help with your sermons and leading worship? Here's an idea…

I heard about *Notebook LM,* a free AI tool by Google, on *The Creative Penn* podcast. (See Links PDF at end.) Author Joanna Penn entered the text of three of her novels into Notebook LM and then played a short extract of the audio interview that the AI generated based on them. I was impressed by the quality of the interview and wanted to try this for myself.

What Notebook LM provided

So, I uploaded the text PDF of my book of 62 collected sermons from 2007-2019 *Let Your Light Shine Through* (see Links PDF at end) into Notebook LM as a source text and asked it to produce an audio interview. The result was amazing! The voices are natural, enthusiastic and engaging.

The man and woman accurately summarised key theological ideas from my sermons, commented on my preaching style and were very positive about my approach to preaching.

I was surprised to have an emotional response to what they said about my sermons. I felt that they "got me" and found the interview affirming and encouraging of my work as a lay preacher. I forgot momentarily that this was produced by an AI.

The first audio (9 minutes) assumed that I was an ordained Methodist minister and referred to me as "Reverend Garside" throughout. I told the

AI that I was a lay preacher not a minister and asked them to refer to me simply as "Philip." I then regenerated the interview.

The second interview (7 minutes) implied that I worked for Wesley Community Action and Winter at Wesley – I don't – so edited out those comments in Audacity. The ending of the second interview was a little flat, so I pasted in the last minute of the first interview which was more upbeat. I then mixed in music at the start and end.

Listen to the edited interview – see Links PDF at end.

Benefits of using Notebook LM

So, how might preachers benefit from using *Notebook LM*?

This tool can help you to assess your overall theology and see the common themes in your sermons.

If you have doubts that your preaching is "Good enough" (we all feel this way sometimes) the AI generated interview will encourage you.

The interview will help you to recognise what you are doing well.

And the interview will spark ideas for topics that you can develop further in future sermons.

Want to try it out?

I suggest that you upload the text of your 10 most recent sermons into Notebook LM. (You do type up your sermons and save/backup the documents – right?)

Combine them into one Word document. Include the title and date at the start of each sermon, and maybe start each sermon on a new page by inserting a page break [CTRL+ENTER]

If you don't have one already, you will first need to set up a Google account. (See Links PDF at end.) Click the *Create an account* link top right.

Then go to the Notebook LM site (see Links PDF at end) and click the *Try Notebook LM* button

Click the + *Create New* button top right. On the next screen upload your document.

Then click *Audio Overview* top right to create your podcast. It will take a few minutes. Then play your interview. You can download the audio as a .wav file. Click the vertical 3 dots.

Fine tuning the Output

You can shape the content of the interview somewhat. Here's the prompt I gave Notebook LM after uploading 11 later sermons:

> "These sermons were written by New Zealand Methodist lay preacher Philip Garside. Refer to him just as "Philip."

> Assume that the audience are church ministers, clergy, lay preachers, worship leaders, church members and spiritual people generally.

> Discuss the key messages in the sermons, the overall theological viewpoint, the sources used in writing the sermons, overall themes that emerge from the sermons, the way Philip engages with the congregation and how the sermons could be improved."

To download the sermons document, I uploaded and the new 19-minute interview that Notebook LM produced see the Links PDF at end.

Other Notebook LM features

As well as generating an interview, try clicking the *Reports* button which will let you generate a *Briefing document, Study Guide, FAQ* and *Timeline* based on your material.

The interactive *Mind Map* and *Video Overview* are also worth trying.

To get help using Notebook LM click the *Settings* button top right, then click *Notebook LM Help.*

15 – Creative Visualisation
– Imagining your movements during a service

This chapter emphasises the importance of visual presence and movement in worship leadership, alongside spoken content. It encourages leaders to plan and visualise their posture, positioning, and transitions throughout the service to maintain connection and avoid jarring moments. Practical tips cover everything from avoiding turning your back to using deliberate movements for emphasis, ensuring the congregation feels guided and engaged.

• • •

Introduction

We rightly spend time carefully preparing our sermons and the rest of the liturgy, selecting the hymns and songs, and creating slide shows to support the service.

But the non-verbal aspects of leading worship are also important. What the congregation *sees* – your posture, presence, and movement – shapes their experience just as much as what they hear. Here are some tips for planning your visual presence thoughtfully and creatively.

You are the visual focus

When training to lead worship, you may have been told something like, "We are worshipping God – it's not about you." While this is good advice about humility and keeping the right attitude towards leading worship, in another way, it isn't quite true.

From before the start of the service through to the end, you are the visual focus for the congregation. At all times, they need to be able to see you. Even when others are leading prayers or giving the children's talk, you provide visual continuity and grounding.

In our church, the worship leader sits in full view at the front – on chairs to the left of the lectern – before the service begins and whenever they are not actively leading.

Sometimes, new worship leaders sit modestly in the second pew, hoping to blend in as one of the congregation. This misunderstands the role. You are there to lead and to *be seen* to be leading. For the duration of the service, you're not simply a member of the congregation – you're guiding the whole experience.

Another unsettling practice I've seen is a preacher sitting hidden in the pulpit while someone else leads prayers or readings, only to pop up and begin preaching. It's jarring for the congregation.

Visualise how you will move during the service

If you're familiar with the church or space where you're leading worship, take a moment during your preparation earlier in the week to visualise your movements. Imagine the whole service in your mind like a movie: where you'll sit, when and where you'll stand, how you'll move between spaces.

If you're unfamiliar with the worship space, spend a few minutes before the service walking through your movements.

Not sure how the offering is collected or brought forward to be blessed? Ask your host or steward for the day.

Planning an interactive children's time? (I hope you are!). Think through where you want the children and adults to stand or move, how you'll handle props, and how you'll re-engage the full congregation afterwards. Pre-thinking their movements as well as yours can help avoid awkward transitions or confusion.

Things I do – and avoid

- I find it valuable to have another congregation member briefly pray with me, in the vestry or other private space, 5-10 minutes before the service starts. This centres me for the task ahead.

- I never fully turn my back to the congregation. At most, I'll quarter-turn away. I learned this from stage acting with Drama Christi.

- During hymns, I step away from the lectern and stand a metre or so to the side, facing the screen. This avoids me doing a solo into the lectern microphone and lets me sing with the congregation.

- After the scripture readings, I rise calmly from my seat beside the lectern and walk across the sanctuary to the pulpit to preach. This moment of gentle theatre creates a visual transition between the readings and sermon. I don't rush or move during the readings.

- When my sermon is finished and before I leave the pulpit, I introduce the next hymn. Then while the organist is playing the introduction I leave the pulpit and walk to my spot beside the lectern ready to sing. This helps continuity.

- When the offering is brought forward, I step from the lectern to the middle level of the sanctuary and lead the blessing. I switch on my lapel microphone beforehand and turn it off afterwards. This provides variety of movement and focus.

- Some past ministers preached without notes and would walk partway up the central aisle to get closer to the congregation. If you can do this well, it draws the congregation in and strengthens the connection.

- I can't preach or pray extemporaneously, (I have tried!), but I do sometimes move forward up the centre aisle when wrapping up the children's talk. It adds emphasis.

- During the benediction or sending forth, I stand at the lectern with arms raised in blessing. This felt strange at first, but it's visually powerful.

- After the Grace, at the very end of the service, I pause and wait for the organist to begin the postlude before walking slowly up the centre aisle to stand at the back of the church. This signals to the congregation that the service is finished. Don't fuss around at the front collecting your notes or bag – you can do that later.

- Final tip: stay standing at the back of the church until everyone who wants to greet you has had the chance. Some will be slow – be patient.

Is your service live-streamed?

If there is live-stream video of your service, at some time in the following week view the recording of the whole service.

What do you notice about your movements and the way you present yourself? What looks good? What could be improved?

Summary

Effective worship leadership isn't just about what you say – it's also about how you move, stand, and hold space. Visual awareness helps the congregation feel calm, connected, and cared for.

Ideas for Worship

Introduction to Ideas for Worship

This section presents a wide-ranging collection of creative, participatory approaches to designing and leading worship.

Worship is an art form that can use movement, storytelling, metaphor, and community collaboration to engage people of all ages. Each chapter outlines a fresh practice or activity – from building a service together in real time, to rewriting parables in modern language, to finding God in everyday experiences like gardens, meals, or music. The emphasis is always on inclusivity, creativity, and honouring diverse voices.

The section highlights the importance of embodiment and symbol in worship. Examples include using circles and spirals as movement-based liturgy, creating tactile rituals, using compost and winter imagery to explore resurrection, or lighting candles and arranging simple displays to connect people with the sacred through physical engagement. These practices help congregation members experience worship not only as words but also through their senses, actions, and shared symbols.

Storytelling and ideas for re-imagining scripture are included, with activities such as collaboratively retelling the Good Samaritan in modern contexts or connecting The Beatles' music and a documentary about them to themes of faith. These examples show how cultural touchpoints, personal experience, and biblical tradition can be woven together to make worship more relevant and emotionally resonant. They encourage worship leaders to notice everyday events, art, and music as potential sparks for worship themes.

The section also provides practical tips to help worship leaders implement these ideas effectively. Suggestions include preparing multiple liturgy options for collaborative services, ensuring accessibility in movement activities, and having contingency plans for technical elements like projection or sound. You don't have to the perfect; rather, creativity, openness, and attentiveness to the Spirit are what make worship meaningful and transformative.

Using Physical Objects

16 – Creating a Natural Treasures Collage

This chapter describes an interactive worship activity where the congregation created a "natural treasures" collage to illustrate 1 Corinthians 12:12-31 and the theme of unity in the church. Using stones, shells, feathers, foliage, and optional candle lighting, participants of all ages contribute to a shared artwork, visually reinforcing the message that each person plays a vital role in the body of Christ. This was a successful as a hands-on, multi-generational way to engage with Scripture.

• • •

Introduction

Looking for a hands-on way to engage people of all ages with a Scripture reading?

Here's an interactive worship activity that encourages participation, reflection, and creativity. (See also chapter 8)

Preparation Before the Service

Set up a long table at the front of the church, ensuring there's space for people to walk around it on all sides. Cover it with a plain tablecloth to provide a neutral background.

On a front pew, arrange a selection of natural treasures in baskets:

- Stones
- Shells
- Feathers
- Freshly cut foliage from your garden (gathered on the day)

To add another dimension, we placed two worn-down beeswax candles from the church cupboard on the pew, along with matches, so people could choose to light them if they wished.

During the Service

After the prayer of approach, but before the Scripture reading, I invited the whole congregation – children and adults – to come forward.

I explained that our reading for the day, 1 Corinthians 12:12-31, speaks of the church as a body with many parts, each working together in unity.

Then, I introduced the activity:

- I invited people to use the materials to create a collage that visually expresses the spirit of unity.
- I reassured them that there was no "right" way to do this – just to place the items as they felt led.

At first, people hesitated. So, to get things rolling, I asked two specific people to start by choosing an item and placing it on the table.

Once they did, others quickly followed, adding materials and shaping the design organically.

Someone asked if they could light the candles, and I said yes.

When the collage was complete, I invited everyone to form a circle around the table. I affirmed the beauty of what they had created and reiterated the message:

Just as each piece contributed to the whole, each person has a place in the church. We need one another to flourish.

While still standing in the circle, we sang the waiata *Wairua Tapu* (See also chapter 28).

Then, everyone returned to their seats.

Reflections on the Experience

Finding an engaging way to introduce the theme in worship – whether as a Time with Children, Story-time, or Introducing the Theme slot – is always a challenge.

The natural treasures collage worked well:

- People of all ages participated, and the hands-on aspect encouraged interaction.
- The Scripture spoke through the activity itself, rather than needing lots of explanation.
- I referenced the collage again later in the sermon, reinforcing its meaning.

Try It for Yourself

Consider ways you could incorporate a similar interactive element in a service you lead.

As an alternative to natural materials, you could use:

- Tools, nails, bolts
- Fabric patches, pottery, buttons
- Toys, playing cards
- Recycled materials, household items…

The key is getting people out of their pews, interacting, and experiencing worship in a tactile way.

You can then explore its meaning more deeply in the sermon.

17 – Visualising the Church Year

This chapter introduces a simple, interactive activity to help congregations – especially children – visualize the flow of the Church Year. By giving volunteers labels of key festivals and arranging them in chronological order, worship leaders can narrate the biblical events and celebrations tied to each season. The exercise concludes with participants forming a circle to illustrate the cyclical nature of the Church Year, making the annual rhythm of worship more memorable and engaging.

• • •

Introduction

As worship leaders, planning services week by week, we are always conscious of which season of the Church Year we are in. But the children and adults in our congregations may not be.

Here's a simple and fun way to explore this.

(I ran this activity some years ago when we were having services in our church hall while the church building was being earthquake strengthened.)

The Activity

Create cards or labels (say four labels per sheet on A4 sheets), which you then cut up, that name the key events and festivals in the church year:

1. Advent
2. Christmas
3. Epiphany
4. Transfiguration
5. Lent
6. Palm Sunday
7. Good Friday
8. Easter Sunday
9. Ascension
10. Pentecost
11. Trinity Sunday

12. Ordinary Time

13. Season of Creation

14. More Ordinary Time

15. Christ the King

To download a PDF with labels for the above 15 items – see Links PDF at end.

If other events in the church calendar are important in your tradition, add them in the appropriate place in the sequence.

Invite the children, (and as many adults as are required to make a total of 15 people) up to the front. Give them each a label to hold and display in front of them.

Ask the person holding the Advent label to come forward and have them stand on the left-hand side of the sanctuary/space. Then ask the person holding the Christmas label to come forward and stand just on the right of the first person.

In this way work through all 15 labels and create a line of people across the sanctuary, standing in chronological order of the Church Year from left to right.

Briefly describe what happened in the Bible at each step and how we celebrate this in church.

Then ask the people holding labels to stay in the same order and form a big circle, so that Advent is standing next to Christ the King. Tell everyone that the Church Year is a repeating cycle.

18 – Worship as Weaving – Threads of Word, Music and Movement

This chapter encourages worship leaders to think of services as woven tapestries rather than linear scripts, interlacing words, music, movement, silence, and story into a unified whole. Using Bill Wallace's hymn *We Are Moving* and a flax weaving activity, it illustrates how worship can embody creativity, interconnection, and communal artistry. Worship as weaving reminds us that leaders are not performers but weavers of meaning, trusting God to bring beauty and strength from the gathered threads.

• • •

Introduction

Good worship doesn't always follow a straight line. It weaves.

It gathers words, music, movement, silence, image, prayer, and story – and interlaces them into something that holds together. Something with strength, texture, flow, and surprise. When we stop seeing services as a checklist and start treating them as tapestries, we create space for the Spirit to be more than just a guest – the Spirit becomes the weaver.

We Are Moving hymn

The image of weaving speaks directly to how worship comes together. It's not just about sequencing. It's about interlacing – letting one thread strengthen and echo another, letting the colours sit next to each other in intentional contrast or harmony.

Bill Wallace's hymn *We Are Moving* expresses this beautifully. To download the PDF sheet music of our arrangement of this hymn – see Links PDF at end.

Verse 3 opens:

> We are weaving, we are weaving, weaving many sacred patterns...
> In a whole that's now emerging, to embrace creative crafting...

This "creative crafting" reminds us that worship is an act of communal artistry. We gather fragments – a Psalm, a story, a silence, a song – and ask, "How might these threads belong together?" The result is not a factory-produced programme, but a handwoven cloth of meaning and movement.

Here's a creative way to embody this idea in worship:

Try a flax weaving activity

Bring strips of harakeke (NZ native flax) into your service. Lay them on a low table or distribute small sets to individuals or groups. As the service progresses – during prayers, song, or reflection – invite people to come forward to the table to weave the strips together.

Give this activity purpose with a question like:

- What threads are you bringing to our worship today?
- What part do you play in the whole?

You don't need to be an expert weaver – even simple overlapping patterns will create something visual and tactile. You could use the resulting mat as a visual centrepiece on your communion table, prayer station, or winter altar (See chapter 38) Let it speak of the interconnection of the Body of Christ.

Weave the hymn itself

After weaving, sing the hymn *We Are Moving* as a response, paying particular attention to verse 3. It reinforces the metaphor and allows people to voice what they've just experienced with their hands and hearts.

Summary

Worship as weaving helps us rethink our role as leaders. We're not performers or producers – we're *weavers of meaning*. We listen, select, and combine with care. And we trust that the final fabric, held in God's hands, will be stronger and more beautiful than we imagined.

Like the best weaving, meaningful worship is strong, textured, and full of grace – created when many threads come together in sacred rhythm.

19 – The Empty Chair
– Praying for the Absent

This chapter introduces the practice of placing an Empty Chair in worship as a symbol for those who are absent – whether due to illness, distance, grief, or death. Congregation members are invited to write names or prayers on slips of paper and place them on the chair, making absence visible and prayerful within the service. Rooted in scripture and easily adapted for different contexts, the Empty Chair becomes a simple yet powerful act of hospitality, memory, and compassion.

• • •

Introduction

In every congregation, there are those who are missing: friends who are ill, family who live far away, people who have drifted from faith, or loved ones who have died.

Their absence is often keenly felt, especially during worship, where community is at the heart of our gathering.

This simple, tactile act of prayer – the Empty Chair – offers a powerful way to honour those absences and bring them prayerfully into the circle of worship.

Setting the Scene

At the front of your worship space, place a single, unoccupied chair. It should be visually distinct – perhaps covered with a special cloth and set apart to signal its purpose.

Introduce the chair early in the service, explaining that it represents those who are not physically present but are still part of our spiritual community.

You might say:

> "This empty chair represents those who are missing today. It stands for our friends and family members who are sick, grieving, travelling, struggling, or simply not with us. It also honours those who have gone before us.
>
> As we continue our worship, you are invited to come forward, take a moment at the chair, and place a note with a name or message on it."

Materials and Participation

Provide small slips of paper and pens or pencils – either on a table nearby or handed out at the start of the service.

Encourage people to write names, a simple prayer, or a brief message such as "Thinking of you" or "Come home soon."

These can be placed directly on the chair.

This physical action allows worshippers to externalize their concerns and prayers in a visible way. The growing pile of notes becomes a testimony to the love and longing that undergirds the community.

It also helps to normalise expressions of absence and grief in a setting that often focuses on presence and joy.

Connecting with Scripture

You might link this action to a scripture such as Luke 15 – the parables of the lost sheep, coin, and son – which all celebrate the return of the absent one.

Or use Paul's words in Philippians 1:3-4: "I thank my God every time I remember you. In all my prayers for all of you, I always pray with joy."

Expanding the Practice

This idea could become a regular part of your worship – perhaps once a month, or during significant liturgical seasons such as Advent, Lent, or All Saints' Day.

It could also be used in small groups or prayer gatherings.

Over time, the empty chair might accumulate a quiet sacredness – a visual reminder of God's care for all, both present and absent.

Conclusion

The Empty Chair gives form to our longing, our concern, and our hope. It reminds us that worship is not only about who is present, but also about holding space for those who cannot be.

In doing so, we practice a deeper kind of hospitality – the hospitality of memory, compassion, and prayer.

20 – Make flax crosses during your Palm-Passion Sunday service

This chapter describes a Palm Sunday activity where worshippers are given flax leaves to wave during hymns and later guided to fold them into crosses. The hands-on practice engages all ages, reinforces the themes of celebration, struggle, and transformation, and deepens connection to the events of Holy Week. With helpers, a demonstration, and a video tutorial, the focus is on participation rather than perfection, making it a meaningful act of shared worship.

• • •

Introduction

Giving congregation members a physical object to hold or pass around helps them to engage with the message of any service.

Here's an idea that I have used successfully in three Palm Sunday services.

Palm Sunday marks the beginning of Holy Week. We remember, and often re-enact, the gospel stories of Jesus riding into Jerusalem on a donkey.

The activity

At the start of the service give people each a flax leaf as they enter the church.

Early in the service sing a joyful hymn and invite people to wave their flax leaves. A good hymn is *Give Me Joy in My heart,* with its uplifting refrain:

> Sing Hosanna! Sing Hosanna!
> Sing Hosanna to the King of kings!
> Sing Hosanna! Sing Hosanna!
> Sing Hosanna to the King!

Later in the service, after the readings and before the sermon, demonstrate to the congregation how to make a flax cross using the flax leaf they waved.

Invite everyone to try to make a cross.

Have some helpers – who can confidently make flax crosses – primed to assist those who need it.

The focus is on attempting to make a cross and joining in the activity, rather than making the most beautiful cross.

This works well as an all-age worship activity.

Instruction video

The YouTube video shows you how to make a flax cross starting with a harvested flax leaf. (See Links PDF at end.)

Project the video in church as people are making their crosses to help them with the process.

Theme

The theme for the services I led was:

Celebration – Struggle – Transformation.

Just as Jesus in Holy Week moved from a joyous demonstration to the horror of the cross, to the mystery of resurrection, so our faith journeys often move from a place of content, to a struggle with new ideas that challenge our earlier beliefs, to a transformed and deeper faith.

Challenge

Try using this activity in your next Palm / Passion Sunday service.

Base your sermon around the meanings that you discover as you explore this idea and practice making crosses.

Further reading

The sermon from a 2013 Palm Sunday service at St Luke's Methodist Church, Pukerua Bay is included in my book *Let Your Light Shine Through* which you can order from us. (See Links PDF at end.)

21 – Hexagons Mosaic
– Many Pieces, One Picture

This chapter introduces an interactive worship activity where each person decorates a paper hexagon with prayers, drawings, or affirmations, then places it on a table to form a collective mosaic. The completed artwork symbolizes unity in diversity, reflecting the Body of Christ as many unique members forming one whole. The mosaic can also be photographed and shared, extending its impact beyond the service.

• • •

Setting the scene

The murmur of voices quiets as you invite everyone – children wriggling free from their parents, teens with shy smiles, adults leaning forward with curiosity – to come to the front. In their hands are small, colourful hexagons, each waiting for a story, a prayer, a splash of colour.

On a table draped with a plain cloth, the beginnings of a mosaic wait. Soon, one by one, people will lay down their pieces, each unique yet perfectly shaped to fit with the others.

Before the service

To create this moment, you'll need to prepare in advance:

- Cut regular hexagons (about 10 cm / 4 inches wide) from thick coloured paper or card in different shades. Precision matters – the more accurately you cut, the better the pieces will fit.
  You can download a free A4 template with six hexagons. (See Links PDF at end.)

- Make enough for every adult and child to have at least one.

- Provide a bucket of marker pens, felt tips, ballpoint pens or soft pencils.

- Either hand them out as people arrive or place the bucket on the front pew or a nearby chair.

- Place a long table (or two together for a large congregation) at the front of the church and cover it with a plain cloth.

During the service

Choose a time such as the Children's Talk or Introducing the Theme slot to begin. Invite everyone forward, asking them to bring their hexagon and pen.

Encourage them to write a short affirmation or prayer, draw a picture, or decorate their hexagon in any way that feels meaningful. They might include the name of someone or a situation they wish to pray for. You can link this activity to your service theme, suggesting ideas to inspire their designs.

Once finished, each person places their hexagon onto the table. Slowly, a mosaic takes shape – a vivid, interconnected picture made from individual pieces.

Then comes the moment of reflection:

- Notice together how each piece is different yet fits snugly with the rest.
- Talk about how this reflects the Body of Christ – many members, one body; many colours, one picture; many prayers, one song of worship.
- Invite people to share their insights or feelings about the activity.

Close with a blessing prayer before sending everyone back to their seats.

Afterwards

Capture the beauty of the mosaic with a photo. Share it on your church's website, social media, or in your next newsletter with a short explanation of its meaning.

For a similar creative all-age worship idea, see chapter 16.

22 – Creative Ways to Mark the Church Seasons with Visual Symbols

This chapter shows how visual and tactile symbols can help congregations engage with the rhythm of the liturgical year. It starts with the traditional colours (purple for preparation, white for joy, red for Spirit, green for growth) and then offers twelve creative ideas beyond pulpit falls and altar cloths. These include banners, candle arrangements, natural elements, seasonal art, interactive tables for children, mobiles, prayer stations, and photo walls.

The key point is that colour and symbol are not just decoration but proclamation – they teach, invite reflection, and enrich worship. Even simple, well-chosen elements can turn ordinary spaces into sacred places of storytelling.

• • •

Simple, meaningful ideas to help your worship space tell the story of the liturgical year

As worship leaders, we're often deeply aware of the rhythms of the Church Year – but how do we help our congregations feel those changes too?

In many churches, colour plays a key role. Here's a typical summary of colours of the church year:

- Purple/Violet: for preparation – Advent and Lent
- White: for light and joy – Christmas, Easter, baptisms, weddings
- Red: for fire and Spirit – Pentecost, ordinations, funerals of highly respected congregation members
- Green: for growth – the 'Ordinary' weeks from Pentecost to Advent

In our church, we use pulpit, and lectern falls and communion tablecloths in these colours to anchor the season visually. But colour can do much more than quietly decorate. With a little creativity, it can preach – teaching, inviting, and deepening the experience of worship.

Here are twelve imaginative and accessible ways to make the liturgical seasons visible and meaningful in your worship space.

1. Banners and Ribbons in Liturgical Colours

Suspend fabric banners or flowing ribbons from the ceiling, across walls, or near the front of the church. Choose rich materials like silk, linen, or satin to add movement and colour that reflects the spirit of each season.

2. Seasonal Candle Displays

Create a candle arrangement that changes with the liturgical cycle:

- Advent: three purple, one pink, and a central white Christ candle
- Lent: six purple or black candles, extinguished weekly
- Easter: white or gold candles to symbolise light and resurrection
- Pentecost: red tea lights or flame-shaped holders

3. Nature on the Communion Table

Bring the outside in with symbols from creation:

- Bare branches or stones during Lent
- Fresh flowers and butterflies at Easter
- Feathers, flames, or wind chimes at Pentecost
- Living plants or bulbs for Ordinary Time

4. Scripture and Symbol Table

Display a focal Bible verse for each season, printed in a beautiful script. Surround it with meaningful symbols – a crown, a lamb, a flame – to help the theme take root visually.

5. Seasonal Art Corner

Invite creative people in your community to contribute art that reflects the season. This could be a painting, a quilt, a piece of sculpture, or even a digital image printed and framed. Change the artwork as the Church Year progresses.

6. Prayer Table with Colour and Texture

Set up a small side table draped in the seasonal colour, with candles, a Bible, or tactile prayer items. This is especially powerful for children, visual learners, and those drawn to quiet contemplation.

7. Church Year Circle Display

Create a large wall-mounted circle showing the liturgical calendar in segments of coloured fabric or card. Use a peg or symbol to mark the current week. Let children help move it each Sunday to reinforce the cycle.

8. Worship Leader Sashes or Scarves

In churches without formal vestments, create simple scarves or stoles in the appropriate colours for lay worship leaders, musicians, or readers to wear – a quiet but meaningful signal of the season.

9. Ceiling Mobiles or Hanging Symbols

Suspend symbols from the ceiling or light fittings:

- Doves, flames, or wind spirals for Pentecost
- Stars or crowns for Epiphany or Christ the King
- Raindrops, leaves, or fish for Creation Season

10. Interactive Children's Table

Set up a weekly table where children (and the young-at-heart) can place or rearrange symbols of the season: rocks for Lent, lilies for Easter, a crown for Christ the King. Change the cloth colour for each season.

11. Multi-Sensory Prayer Stations

Especially during Lent, Advent, or the Season of Creation, invite the congregation to visit small prayer stations using colour, sound, scent, or touch:

- A bowl of sand (wilderness)
- Anointing oil (blessing)
- Shells or water (baptism)
- A bell and silence (centring)

12. Seasonal Photo Wall

Invite people to share photos that symbolise the current season, e.g.

- Sunrise for Easter
- Autumn leaves for Creation
- A lit candle in darkness for Advent

Print and display them in matching frames in seasonal colours.

Summary

By layering in visual and tactile elements, we give the whole congregation a chance to see the gospel unfold. These symbols don't need to be expensive or elaborate.

A few well-chosen colours, textures, or shapes can stir imagination, deepen reflection, and turn ordinary worship spaces into sacred storytelling places.

(See also chapter 17)

23 – Folding Faith – Worship with Origami

This chapter explores how origami can be used as a reflective, hands-on practice in worship, turning simple paper folds into prayers and symbols of faith. Different shapes like boxes, doves, boats, hearts, and stars can represent themes such as peace, trust, love, and hope. In particular, the origami box offers rich possibilities for worship, serving as a container for prayers, blessings, spiritual gifts, or symbols of God's holding presence.

• • •

The Idea

Sometimes the most profound moments in worship come not through words, but through stillness, touch, and focused movement.

Origami – the ancient Japanese art of paper folding – offers a beautiful, reflective practice that fits perfectly within Christian worship. During a service, invite people to fold a square of paper into a meaningful shape: a box, a dove, a heart, a boat… Each fold becomes a prayer, a movement of transformation.

It's worship that forms in the hands – simple, symbolic, and sacred.

Why Origami?

Origami slows us down. It invites us to be present. A flat square becomes something more – not instantly, but through care, patience, and willingness to be shaped.

Isn't that the Christian journey too?

Theologically, origami offers a metaphor for how God forms us: through gentle, intentional shaping. And practically, it provides an easy, multi-sensory activity for all ages that can be used in services, small groups, retreats, and intergenerational gatherings.

Which Symbol to Fold?

Some ideas for shapes:

- Box – for prayer, holding, offering, or unexpected gifts (see below)
- Dove – for peace, Pentecost, or the baptism of Jesus
- Boat – for trust, storms, or being called to follow

- Heart – for love, forgiveness, or community
- Star – for guidance, Epiphany, or hope in darkness

Choose a simple folding pattern that's achievable in a group setting.

See Links PDF at end for YouTube videos showing how to fold these shapes:

- Box
- Dove
- Boat
- Heart
- Star

How to Use Origami in Worship

- Distribute the materials – squares of paper, possibly with scripture or words printed on one side.
- Explain the symbol and context – What does the shape represent today? Why use this symbol?
- Guide the folding process – Lead it during a sermon, prayer, or reflection. Use pauses between steps to invite thought or silence. Ideally project the relevant YouTube video in your church. Pause the video after each step so the congregation can make their folds and creases.
- Reflect and share – Invite people to bring their completed shapes forward as an offering, pin them to a wall, or take them home as a spiritual reminder.

An Origami Box: 8 Ways to Use It

The box is especially rich in metaphor and liturgical use. Here are eight ideas for incorporating it into worship:

1. A Container for Prayer or Gratitude
Invite people to write prayers or thanksgivings and place them in their box. Collectively, these can be displayed or offered during prayer.

2. Symbol of God's Holding Presence
Reflect on how God holds our lives with care. Boxes represent being safely held, echoing scriptures like "You hem me in, behind and before." (Psalm 139:5)

3. The Manger at Christmas

Use the box as a symbol of the manger – simple, open, expectant. Invite people to place something inside as a sign of welcoming Christ.

4. God's Surprising Gifts

Boxes can be used to represent spiritual gifts or blessings. Place cards with words like "peace", "joy", or "wisdom" inside, to be discovered.

5. Limits and Liberation

Use the box to reflect on how we try to "contain" God. Then unfold or open it symbolically, representing liberation, openness, and mystery.

6. Lenten Letting Go

Have people place inside their box something symbolic they are letting go of during Lent – a worry, habit, or burden.

7. What's in Your Box?

Invite reflection on identity, calling, or gifts. "What do I carry? What do I offer?" Boxes become a metaphor for our own inner journey.

8. Blessing Exchange

Have each person write a blessing and place it in someone else's box anonymously. Everyone leaves worship with a gift of encouragement.

Summary

When we fold paper together in worship, we shape more than symbols – we shape stories, prayers, and moments of grace. The humble origami box, held in a worshipper's hand, becomes a space where God meets us – holding what we bring, transforming what we offer.

24 – The Sound of Stones
– Rhythm and Storytelling in Worship

This chapter shows how ordinary stones can become powerful tools for worship, creating rhythm, soundscapes, and prayerful reflection without traditional instruments. By clicking, rubbing, or dropping stones, congregations can add heartbeat-like rhythm to psalms, dramatize scripture stories, or embody intercessory prayers. Simple yet profound, stones connect worshippers to ancient biblical symbolism and the grounding presence of creation itself.

• • •

The Idea

Worship doesn't always need keyboards or guitars to be musical. Sometimes all you need is what you can hold in your hand.

Give each person two small, smooth stones (get them from a local beach, river or garden/landscaping supplies store).

Ask them to hold a stone in each hand and gently repeatedly bang the stones together to make a clicking sound. This sets up a shared rhythm – click, click, click, click.

The stones will become a shared heartbeat for a Psalm read aloud together, or to punctuate a bible story. The words will pulse with sound. People will discover that silence too has a texture. Worship can became not just spoken or sung but *felt*.

This is the invitation: use stones as instruments of rhythm, reflection, and response. Their simplicity makes them accessible for all ages and settings.

Why stones?

Stones are ancient. Biblical. Sacred. From the stone Jacob used as a pillow, to the ones the crowd would have thrown at the woman caught in adultery, to the rolled-away stone at Jesus' tomb – they carry metaphor, weight, and memory.

And they can fit in our hands. Their solidity grounds us. Their sound – when struck together, tapped on wood, or shaken in a jar – gives voice to the unspeakable. Joy. Lament. Longing.

How to use them in worship

1. Psalm with Pulse
Choose a Psalm with strong rhythm and repetition – like Psalm 136. Invite the congregation to read it aloud rhythmically and *click their stones* on each strong syllable, e.g. "God's **stead**fast **love** en**dures** for**ever**". Click twice at the end of each line. [Demonstrate this for the congregation before they start reading.] The stones become both a beat and an embodied "Amen."

2. Soundscape for a Story
Tell a dramatic scripture story – such as the crossing of the Red Sea or the road to Emmaus. Invite participants to make sounds with their stones at key points:

- Tapping slowly for walking
- Rubbing stones together for murmuring crowds
- Loud claps for moments of surprise or divine intervention.

This works especially well with intergenerational groups, as it draws even shy participants into the moment.

3. Prayer with Pebbles
Give each person a handful of small pebbles. During the intercessory prayers, invite them to pick up and drop back into their hand a stone for each person or place they name silently. The movement and sound offer a gentle, embodied symbolic action.

Summary
Let the stones cry out – not in protest, but in praise, rhythm, and prayer – grounding your worship in the sound and touch of the earth.

25 – What's in Your Pocket?
– Everyday Faith Objects

This chapter introduces a creative worship practice that helps people discover spiritual meaning in the everyday items they carry in their pockets or bags. By reflecting on objects like keys, coins, or receipts, worshippers are invited to see them as symbols of faith, trust, and daily discipleship. The activity reminds us that God is present not only in church rituals but also in the ordinary details of our daily lives.

• • •

Introduction – Discovering the Sacred in the Ordinary

Worship doesn't always require special objects or elaborate rituals.

Meaningful insights can also come from the items we carry with us every day – keys, receipts, coins, tissues, lip balm.

This interactive worship idea encourages your congregation to explore how these seemingly mundane objects can symbolize deeper truths about faith and life.

The Setup – An Invitation to Reflect

Partway through the service, invite everyone to reach into their pockets, purses, or bags and pull out a single item – anything they happen to be carrying. Then ask:

> "What might this object say about your faith journey, or your relationship with God? What could it symbolize?"

Give people a moment to reflect quietly on their item.

Then offer the chance for a few to share with the group, either by speaking aloud or writing down a short reflection to be read anonymously.

Examples to Get People Started

Some members of your congregation may need help thinking symbolically. Share a few examples to inspire them:

- A bunch of keys might symbolize security, trust, or unlocking possibilities.

- A handkerchief could signify compassion, healing, or the presence of tears and comfort.

- A credit card may point to responsibility, provision, or the way we spend and steward our resources.

- A pen might reflect the importance of communication or how God is still writing our story.

- A coin could suggest value, generosity, or life's choices.

- A mobile phone may represent connection, distraction, or a means of spiritual community.

- A receipt might highlight our habits, gratitude, or the small daily blessings we often overlook.

Encourage people to be playful and imaginative, as well as thoughtful.

Scriptural Connection – Everyday Parables

You might link this activity with passages where Jesus used everyday objects to teach profound truths:

- A mustard seed (Matthew 13:31-32)
- A coin (Luke 15:8-10)
- A fig tree (Mark 11:12-14)
- A lamp (Matthew 5:14-16)

These remind us that nothing is too small or ordinary to hold spiritual significance.

Expanding the Idea – A Pocket Display

To create a visual and symbolic centrepiece, invite people to place their item – such as a phone, receipt, keyring, or coin – on a central table or communion table as a temporary offering.

These are not left behind but simply placed there for the duration of the service as a shared expression of faith through everyday life.

Let the table quietly speak of how faith and ordinary life are deeply intertwined.

Before the final blessing, invite people to come forward and collect their objects.

As they do so, say something like:

"As we return these everyday items to our pockets and purses, we carry more than objects – we carry renewed awareness of God in all things. May these small symbols remind us to live out our faith in the everyday world."

This simple ritual connects worship with life outside the church walls.

Conclusion – Faith That Travels with Us

This worship activity helps people see that faith isn't confined to Sunday morning.

It's present in every pocket and purse, woven into the fabric of daily life.

The objects we carry reveal where we've been, what we need, and what we value.

They remind us that God is with us, not just in sacred spaces, but everywhere we go.

26 – Footprints of Faith
– Discerning God's direction in our lives

Discover a creative, all-age worship activity using footprint cut-outs to reflect on spiritual journeys and God's guidance. This interactive exercise invites participants to write prayerful intentions on footprints, forming a symbolic path of faith. Perfect for deepening community reflection and exploring where God is calling each of us next.

• • •

Walking with God – Together

Life is full of movement – sometimes forward, sometimes uncertainly sideways, and occasionally in circles!

As people of faith, we often speak of "walking with God", "following Jesus", or "being led by the Spirit."

But how often do we pause to reflect on where we *are* on that journey – and where we feel called to go next?

This simple yet meaningful activity uses cut-outs of feet to explore the metaphor of faith as a journey. It's interactive, reflective, and visually striking – ideal for all-age worship.

Preparation

Before the service, cut out pairs of footprints: a left and right foot for each person. Thin card works best, but paper is fine too.

- Download a free A4 PDF template to print or photocopy – see Links PDF at end.

You will also need pens or markers.

During the Service

Introduction

After a reading or reflection on biblical journeys (e.g. Abraham's call in Genesis 12, the Exodus, Jesus calling the disciples, or Paul's missionary travels), invite the congregation to consider their own spiritual journey.

You might say:

> "God has always called people to move – from comfort to courage, from fear to faith, from the familiar to the unknown. Today, we pause to ask: Where is God calling me to go next?"

Action
Distribute the pairs of footprint cut-outs. Invite people to take a moment of quiet, then write on each foot where they sense God is leading them. One foot might say "more patience," the other "speak up for justice." One might say "be still," and the other "trust more deeply."

Encourage balance: two feet, two directions that work together. This might reflect inner and outer change, or intention and action.

Creating the Pathway
Once people have written their responses, invite them (one by one or in small groups) to walk up the aisle and lay their footprints down on the floor in a line, heel-to-toe. Over the course of the activity, a pathway of prayerful intentions and faithful hopes will emerge – leading right into the sanctuary or towards the communion table.

This physical path symbolises our collective movement toward God's future, step by step.

Optional Variations
- Play instrumental music or a walking-themed hymn during the placement of footprints.

- Invite people to walk the path after it's been laid, prayerfully reading the footprints.

- Take photos of the completed path and share them as a visual devotion later.

- Include children by having them decorate the footprints with colours or stickers as a symbol of joy and creativity in their faith journeys.

- At the end of the service, allow people to take home one footprint (not their own) as a reminder to pray for another's journey during the coming week.

Closing Reflection

To conclude, say something like:

> "These are not just pieces of paper. They are your prayers, your intentions, your faithful steps into the unknown.
>
> May this path remind us that we walk together, and that God walks with us, every step of the way."

Music and Songs

27 – *Kindle a Flame*
– One song, many uses

This chapter introduces *Kindle a Flame*, a simple, reflective worship song written by the author, which can be used in services, small groups, or personal devotions. Its repetitive verses make it adaptable for prayer responses, candle-lighting liturgies, or as a unifying sung meditation. With flexible performance options and free downloadable resources, the song invites worshippers to embody light, justice, hope, love, and peace in their lives.

• • •

About this Song

I wrote *Kindle a Flame* as a reflective song for worship, and I have used it many times when leading services. It also works well as part of the devotions for a small group, and as an individual, private meditation (change "our hearts" to "my heart").

The words are simple and repetitive.

Here are the words of the full song.

Kindle a flame

Kindle a flame within our hearts
let your *light* shine through
let your *light* shine through.

Kindle a flame within our hearts
let your *justice* shine through
let your *justice* shine through.

Kindle a flame within our hearts
let your *hope* shine through
let your *hope* shine through.

Kindle a flame within our hearts
let your *love* shine through
let your *love* shine through.

Kindle a flame within our hearts
let your *peace* shine through
let your *peace* shine through.

How to sing / perform the song

Keep the instrumentation very simple.

When accompanying on guitar, just pluck the chords, or use a gentle, steady arpeggio picking style. If you want to strum, just play one down strum for each chord.

Flute or recorder would be great to teach people the tune first and then to support the singing.

Once you know the song, try singing unaccompanied.

Free Downloads

See Links PDF at end to download:

- the PDF sheet music.
- a midi file of the melody – 5 verses
- an MP3 file of the melody – 5 verses
- a Noteworthy Composer (2.75) setting

Using the song in worship

You can sing the song right through – all five verses.

You can use just the first verse as a sung response to intercessory prayer petitions, i.e. leader speaks a stanza of prayer, and the people sing the response.

You can use all 5 verses in a prayer. The first petition focuses on light and then the people respond by singing verse 1. The second petition focuses on justice, and the people respond by singing verse 2, and so on…

As a spoken, responsive liturgy. Here is a re-working of the song for use as a candle lighting liturgy. You will notice that verses 4 and 5 have been swapped around.

Lighting the candles – liturgy

As we light these candles:

Kindle a flame within our hearts, O God
and let your light shine through

Kindle a flame within our hearts, O God
and let your justice shine through

Kindle a flame within our hearts, O God
and let your hope shine through

Kindle a flame within our hearts, O God
and let your peace shine through

Kindle a flame within our hearts, O God
and let your love shine through. Amen.

Matching Benediction/Sending forth

If you have used the song or liturgy during the service, try using this Benediction to close the service:

Loving God,
our time of worship today has now ended.
As we leave this sacred space,
we carry in our hearts the flame of your love,
the spark of the holy spirit,
out into the world. Amen.

You can order the PDF eBook in which this song appears from us – *Kindle A Flame: Songs, Prayers & Poems: Creative Worship Volume 1.* (See Links PDF at end.)

28 – *Loving God of Aotearoa*
– A Hymn for Unity, Service and Creation

This hymn celebrates unity in diversity, compassionate service, and God's presence in the beauty of creation. Its verses honour past faithful people, draw on imagery of rimu trees, tui song, and Matariki, and call the church to forgiveness and new beginnings. Designed for both worship and reflection, the hymn provides a rich resource for congregational singing, thematic focus, and community engagement.

• • •

About the hymn

I wrote *Loving God of Aotearoa* for the late Rev Desmond Cooper for his induction as President of the Methodist Church in 2010.

It is part of my PDF eBook *Kindle A Flame*, a collection of songs, hymns and prayers. (To order See Links PDF at end.)

The hymn offers a rich tapestry of theological and cultural elements that resonate deeply within the context of both the Methodist and wider church in New Zealand.

Here are the words:

1. Loving God of Aotearoa,
   hear now our call to you,
   We have gathered in your presence,
   to celebrate anew!
   We have come from many places,
   speaking, thinking differently,
   But in you we are united,
   one whole, strong family.

   Refrain:
   Let us heed your call to service
   and follow lovingly,
   May we be compassionate people,
   alive in you and free.

2. Scripture tells of faithful people,
    who spread your light and love.
    Now inspire, lead, direct us,
    so we can be like them.
    May the Way that Christ has taught us,
    and the power of your Word,
    Set a fire burning in us,
    for justice and for love.

3. Rimu tall, with tui singing,
    proclaim your majesty,
    You who care for all creation,
    will always care for me.
    Matariki's spirit guide us,
    rise within us all the year.
    Help us live and speak forgiveness,
    your people want to hear.

To download a sheet music setting See Links PDF at end.

Key themes of the hymn

- **Unity in Diversity:** The hymn begins by acknowledging the diverse nature of the church in Aotearoa New Zealand, where people from various backgrounds, with differing thoughts and languages, come together as one united family under the love of God. This theme of unity is central to the hymn's message, emphasising that despite differences, a shared faith binds the congregation together.

- **A Call to Compassionate Service:** The refrain, "Let us heed your call to service and follow lovingly, May we be compassionate people, alive in you and free," directly echoes the message of one of my sung prayer responses – *Happy are we who have work to do* – by issuing a call to action. It emphasises the responsibility of Christians to actively serve others with love and compassion, embodying Christ's teachings in their daily lives.

- **Honouring Past Faithful People:** Verse 2 draws inspiration from those who have faithfully served God in the past, urging the congregation to follow their example. By acknowledging the legacy of faithful individuals, the hymn encourages a sense of continuity and commitment to carrying forward the torch of faith and service.

- **God's Presence in Aotearoa's Natural Beauty:** Verse 3 shifts the focus to the majestic presence of God in the natural world, using imagery specific to Aotearoa New Zealand. The towering rimu trees, the melodious tui birdsong, and the celestial guidance of Matariki, the Māori New Year star cluster, all point to God's creative power and loving care for all creation. (Worship leaders in other countries may want to use alternative imagery that reflects their land.)

- **Forgiveness and New Beginnings:** The hymn concludes by linking Matariki's symbolism of new beginnings to the act of giving and receiving forgiveness. This connection emphasises the transformative power of forgiveness, allowing individuals and communities to leave behind past hurts and embrace a future filled with hope and freedom.

Guiding Worship: Integrating *Loving God of Aotearoa* into Services

This hymn's rich thematic content and evocative imagery provide worship leaders with a powerful tool for enriching church services. Here are several ways to effectively incorporate it:

- **Congregational Singing:** *Loving God of Aotearoa* can be sung by the entire congregation as a hymn of praise and commitment to God. Its straightforward melody and clear lyrics make it accessible for all ages and singing abilities.

- **Thematic Focus:** The hymn can be used to support sermons or reflections focusing on themes of unity, service, creation care, or forgiveness. Its lyrics provide a scriptural and cultural foundation for exploring these concepts in depth.

- **Visual Enhancements:** Incorporating visuals during the singing of this hymn can deepen its impact. Images of Aotearoa's natural beauty, such as rimu forests, tui birds, or the Matariki star cluster, can visually connect the congregation to the hymn's message.

- **Responsive Reading:** The verses can be read responsively, with a leader reading the first line of each verse and the congregation responding with the remaining lines. This approach emphasises the call and response nature of the hymn and encourages active listening.

Performance Considerations

- **Key and Accompaniment:** The hymn is best sung in its original key (or a slightly lower one) and accompanied by piano or organ to preserve its intended melodic and harmonic richness.

- **Word Emphasis:** Encourage clear enunciation of the word "compassionate" in the refrain, as it spans three notes and requires careful articulation.

- **Tempo and Dynamics:** Maintain a moderate tempo that allows the congregation to fully engage with the text.

Beyond the Service

Here are a couple ways you can use *Loving God of Aotearoa* beyond the confines of a church service:

- **Small Group Discussions:** Use the hymn as a starting point for discussions on unity, service, and creation care in small group settings.
  Encourage participants to share their personal reflections on the hymn's message and how it applies to their lives.

- **Community Outreach:** The hymn's call to compassionate service can inspire action.
  Encourage the congregation to identify needs within their community and find ways to serve others with love and generosity.

Summing up

By thoughtfully incorporating *Loving God of Aotearoa* into worship services and beyond, worship leaders can inspire their congregations to embrace a deeper connection with God, their community, and the awe-inspiring beauty of Aotearoa New Zealand.

The hymn serves as a reminder of the importance of unity, service, and the enduring presence of God in the natural world.

29 – Singing Waiata in English-Language Services

This chapter explores how singing waiata (Māori hymns or songs) in English-language services can enrich worship by honouring te reo Māori, deepening cultural and theological understanding, and fostering inclusivity. It outlines both the benefits and challenges of incorporating waiata, including issues of language, pronunciation, authenticity, and accessibility of meaning. Two waiata – *He Hōnore* and *Wairua Tapu* – are introduced as powerful, spiritually resonant songs that can be used year-round to connect congregations with Māori spirituality and Christian faith.

• • •

Introduction

Singing waiata (Māori hymns or songs) in English-language church services is a meaningful way to honour te reo Māori and incorporate indigenous spirituality into worship.

It deepens the cultural and theological richness of services and acknowledges the bi-cultural commitments of many churches in Aotearoa New Zealand.

This chapter discusses:

- The benefits and challenges of singing waiata in English-language services
- Whether English language translations should be provided
- The subtle musical nature of waiata, and
- Introduces two waiata that we sing at our church – *He Hōnore* and *Wairua Tapu* – which have become a loved part of our worship repertoire and are suitable for singing any time of year.

Benefits and challenges

Introducing waiata into worship also presents both benefits and challenges.

Six Benefits of Singing Waiata in Worship

- **Honouring te reo Māori**: Incorporating waiata respects and upholds the indigenous language of Aotearoa New Zealand, fostering greater appreciation and engagement with Māori culture.

- **Encouraging Inclusivity and Reconciliation:** Singing waiata in church acknowledges the Treaty of Waitangi and strengthens relationships between Māori and non-Māori worshippers.

- **Enriching Worship with Māori Theology:** Waiata often contain deep theological themes rooted in Māori spirituality, bringing fresh insights into the nature of God and faith.

- **Deepening Congregational Participation:** Learning and singing waiata can create a more engaged worship experience, moving people beyond words to shared spiritual meaning.

- **Developing Musical and Cultural Competency:** Singing waiata helps congregations grow musically by learning different rhythms, melodies, and harmonies specific to Māori musical traditions.

- **Creating a Sense of Unity:** Singing in te reo together fosters communal identity, reinforcing the shared faith and mutual respect among worshippers.

Six Challenges of Singing Waiata in Worship

- **Language Barrier:** Some congregation members may be unfamiliar with te reo Māori, making it difficult to engage fully in the meaning of the waiata.

- **Pronunciation Difficulties:** Proper pronunciation is essential to show respect and accurately convey meaning. This can take time and practice to learn.

- **Theological Understanding:** Some congregation members may struggle to grasp the full depth of Māori theological perspectives embedded in waiata without contextual explanation.

- **Musical Complexity:** Waiata often have subtle rhythms and syncopation that, while appearing simple, require careful musical notation and rehearsal to perform well.

- **Resistance to Change:** Some church members may feel uncomfortable incorporating non-English elements into worship. Worship leaders need to navigate this thoughtfully.

- **Ensuring Authenticity and Respect:** Using waiata appropriately means engaging with Māori perspectives and ensuring the songs are presented in a way that honours their origins.

Should English Translations Be Provided?

One common question is whether to provide an English translation for waiata or encourage congregation members to seek out meanings themselves.

Some argue that providing translations allows for greater understanding and accessibility, helping non-Māori speakers engage more deeply with the worship experience.

Others believe that not providing a translation encourages people to become more familiar with te reo Māori, respecting its status as a living language rather than treating it as something that needs to be mediated through English.

Churches might consider striking a balance – perhaps offering an initial translation when introducing a waiata but encouraging deeper learning over time.

The Musical Nature of Waiata

Waiata often appear deceptively simple but have intricate musical elements that require careful attention. (For example, see the PDF sheet music for *Wairua Tapu* which has triplets, notes tied across beats, and varied note lengths.)

The subtle rhythms, syncopations, and natural flow of te reo Māori syllables demand precise musical notation and dedicated rehearsal.

Without proper preparation, a congregation may struggle to maintain the fluidity and spiritual depth of the song.

Choirs and musicians who lead congregations in singing waiata should work closely with native speakers or experienced waiata singers to ensure they capture both the musical and cultural essence of the songs.

Introducing Two Waiata

He Hōnore

Music: Taina Piripi Ngarimu (c. 1992)
Words: Ringatū prayer based on Luke 2:14

He hōnore, he korōria,
Maungārongo ki te whenua,
Whakaaro pai e ki ngā tāngata katoa,
Ake, ake, ake, ake, Āmine.
Te Atua, Te piringa,
Toku oranga, Toku oranga.

Honour, glory,
Peace on earth,
Goodwill to all people,
Forever and ever, Amen.
God is my refuge,
My salvation, my life.

This waiata reflects the angelic proclamation of Luke 2:14, affirming the themes of peace, goodwill, and divine refuge. It captures a universal Christian message while emphasising the Māori concept of piringa (refuge), resonating with the idea of God as a sheltering presence.

We sing the waiata through twice, raising the melody by a tone the second time round.

Wairua Tapu

Words & Music: Dr. Ngāpō (Bub) Wehi c. 1994

Wairua tapu tau mai rā,
Wairua tapu mai runga,
Uhia mai ngā taonga pai,
Homai tō aroha,
Wahia ka tika,
Akona mai rā kia ū ki te pai,
Horohia kia mau tonu rā,
Mōhou te tino korōria.

Holy Spirit, descend upon us,
Holy Spirit from above,
Bestow upon us Your good gifts,
Give us Your love,
Break through in righteousness,
Teach us to hold fast to what is good,

Spread Your presence so it remains,
For Yours is the ultimate glory.

This waiata is an invocation of the Holy Spirit, emphasising divine presence, transformation, and righteousness. It aligns closely with Pentecostal themes while carrying the depth of Māori spirituality, which understands wairua (spirit) as an active, guiding force.

We sing the waiata through twice, then end by repeating the first line three times, gradually getting slower and fading out.

Summary

Introducing waiata into English-language church services is a way to honour te reo Māori, enrich worship, and foster cultural understanding.

While challenges exist, they can be overcome through education, practice, and openness to learning.

Whether to provide English translations is a nuanced question, but encouraging deeper familiarity with te reo fosters greater respect and appreciation.

With careful preparation and sensitivity, churches can ensure that singing waiata becomes a meaningful and spiritually enriching part of their worship life.

Downloads

See Links PDF at end to download these resources.

He Hōnore:

- a PDF melody line setting with chords
- a midi file
- an MP3 audio recording of the waiata being sung in our church.

Wairua Tapu:

- a PDF melody line setting with chords
- a midi file
- an MP3 audio recording of the waiata being sung in our church.

30 – Three Easy Sung Responses to Enrich Your Worship

This chapter encourages worship leaders to replace spoken prayer responses with simple sung ones, creating deeper unity and engagement in services. It offers three original sung responses, each with practical guidance for use, including tips on rounds, modulation, and combining silence with song. These responses are designed to be flexible, memorable, and spiritually enriching for communal prayer.

• • •

Introduction

In worship, sometimes a simple adjustment can deepen engagement and create a more memorable experience for the congregation.

Here's a fresh approach to try in your next service: instead of a spoken prayer response, try singing it!

Sung responses add a sense of unity and reverence to communal prayer, allowing everyone to participate actively.

Here are three sung responses I've written and used in my services, along with tips for integrating them effectively into worship.

How to Use These Responses

After each stanza of prayer, invite the congregation to join in singing a response.

Alternate between spoken word and sung response to create a rhythm, drawing people into the moment.

These responses can be accompanied by guitar, piano, organ, flute, or any available instruments, but they also work well unaccompanied.

Here are some tips:

- **Learn the melody:** You don't have to be perfect. Set the pitch at a comfortable level for your voice.
- **Prime a couple of strong singers** in the congregation who can lead the way, encouraging others to join in.

- **Try a meditative style** by singing the response and allowing a full minute of silence before singing it again. Repeat these two or three times. This gives space for personal reflection.

- **Sing in rounds:** For *Happy Are We*, try a two-part round where one group starts, then another joins in a bar later. For a round everyone should sing the whole response at least three times. Singing in rounds adds texture and depth to the experience.

- **Modulate for variation:** Sing the response once, then repeat it a tone or two higher. This will feel uplifting.

- **Interspersed prayer:** Sing the first phrase, offer a prayer, and follow with the second phrase to weave sung response with spoken word.

See Links PDF at end for a short video of me singing the responses and an MP3 audio file of me singing the responses

1. Happy Are We Who Have Work to Do, Come and Help Us Serve the Lord

Happy are we who have work to do

In the Methodist tradition we have a Covenant Service early in the year to affirm the missional work we will do and commit to each other as a team of clergy and lay church members for the coming year. Typically, this is the first Sunday in February when people are back from summer holidays and if there have been changes of ministers, the new clergy are in place, having moved during January.

For this service, I wrote a Covenant Song. After trying the song in a service, I wasn't happy with the verses and set them aside. But the refrain works well.

Sung as a round or on repeat, this response is a meaningful reminder of our shared purpose and commitment to serve together.

2. Lamb of God, You Take Away the Sin of the World, Have Mercy on Us

Lamb of God (from A Hopkins Gloria)

Words: NZ Prayerbook   Music: Jonathan Berkahn (2019) (Adapted)

Lamb of God, you take a-way the sin of the world:

have mer-cy on us.

Translated from the traditional *Agnus Dei* text in the Latin mass, this response brings an ancient reverence to modern worship.

Lean into the word "sin," highlighting the sharpened note for drama and emphasis. This response is well-suited for a Prayer of Confession or Prayer of Approach, followed by Words of Assurance.

Wellington composer Jonathan Berkahn wrote a choral work, *A Hopkins Gloria*, for our choir Festival Singers, inspired by Gerard Manley Hopkins' text. I adapted this response from part of his work.

(To order a digital recording of *A Hopkins Gloria* see the Links PDF at end.)

3. Living God's Love, Acting for the Common Good

This response is based on our congregation's vision statement, crafted a couple of years ago by our leaders.

Living God's Love

Text: 10am Leaders Group   Tune: Philip & Heather Garside

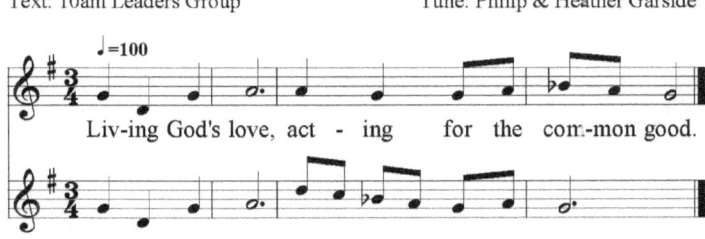

Liv-ing God's love, act - ing   for the com-mon good.

Liv-ing God's love, act-ing for the com-mon good.

The tune I started with for the second phrase was boring, and Heather suggested the falling line you see now. Much better!

Railways

31 – Railways as metaphors 1
– *People Get Ready*

This chapter uses the song *People Get Ready* as a springboard for exploring how trains can serve as rich metaphors for faith and worship. It offers practical ways to incorporate the song into a service, from printed lyrics and video playback to small-group discussion linking the imagery to God's grace and the journey of faith. The key takeaway for worship leaders is to keep filling their kete with diverse cultural experiences so they can draw on them as fresh, engaging illustrations in worship.

• • •

Introduction

When rock guitarist Jeff Beck died in early 2023, I was reminded of a lovely song I found on YouTube some years earlier of him playing and Rod Stewart singing – *People Get Ready* (Words and Music: Curtis Mayfield).

For the YouTube video, which includes the lyrics in the details below the video, see the Links PDF at end.

How does this relate to leading worship in church? Let's find out…

Comments and questions

I saw Rod Stewart perform live at Athletic Park here in Wellington around 1979-80. His was one of the most memorable concerts I have been to because he engaged so well with the audience. He has a distinctive voice and relaxed way of singing. (He is also a skilled railway modeller!)

I really like Jeff Beck's guitar work on this recording. His solos complement the singing, are melodic and not flashy. His playing serves the song. Notice towards the end of the song how he modulates up a key, which gives a boost and new life to the song, even as the band is playing out.

How could you use this song in worship?

Give the congregation the lyrics in print in the Order of Service, or on separate sheets, so they can see all three verses at once.

You could ask the congregation to say the lyrics aloud as a reading.

If you have an audio-visual system, play the YouTube video. Or just play the audio through your sound system.

Having played the song, ask the congregation to spend 5 minutes discussing the recording and the lyrics with people in the pews/seats next to them.

- What did they like?
- What were they surprised by?
- Did the visuals in the video help tell a story?
- How might boarding the train in the song relate to our spiritual, faith journeys?
- What does the song teach or remind us about God's grace, and how we should respond to it?
- Is there room for sinners in God's Kingdom / the Realm of God?

At the end of the discussion time, ask people to share their thoughts and insights with the whole congregation.

As the worship leader, you should prepare some comments and insights of your own and be ready to share them. This could lead into your sermon.

Key learning for worship leaders

Keep filling your mental worship *kete*/basket.

Be open to new experiences, music, video / films / documentaries, art and books. Be aware of what is happening in your communities and in the world – not just the headlines but also the underlying social trends.

Then when the time is right you can draw from your *kete* a spark to illustrate the key message in your next service. You'll never be short of things to say when leading worship.

32 – Railways as metaphors 2
– Layers of meaning

This chapter reflects on a 2014 service where a steam train journey with my father became a metaphor for exploring the multiple layers of meaning in Bible stories. The train trip illustrated how narratives can be understood at the level of context, events, surface meaning, and deeper spiritual insight, leading to lessons about relationships, shared experiences, and enjoying the journey. Applied to scripture, such as the Feeding of the Five Thousand, this layered approach reveals Eucharistic symbolism and challenges us to embody Jesus' call to "give them something to eat" in today's world.

• • •

Introduction

This chapter is based on a service which I led in 2014. I explored the idea that Bible stories have multiple layers of meaning, using the story of a steam train trip my dad Paul and I took earlier that year. I showed a short video I made of the trip.

Introducing the Theme (2014)

"In a moment I'm going to show you some photos and video I took when my Dad Paul and I went on a trip from Christchurch to Greymouth and back again on a steam train. I took 379 photos and 2 hours of video... but you will be pleased to know I have kept this morning's presentation down to just under 4 minutes. This is the first of the three stories we will consider.

One of the challenges of preaching is to identify, understand and share the deeper meanings of the stories and passages in our lectionary scripture readings. I heard recently about a Christian who asked the Dalai Lama whether she should become a Buddhist to gain a deeper sense of God. He answered no, you should delve deeper into the mysteries of your own faith. A wise answer.

It seems to me that stories have four layers.

- First there are the background, context, social conditions, and location of the story. John Dominic Crossan calls this – Matrix. I like that. We need to know how the story came to be told.

- Second there is the story itself – the narrative layer. Characters say and do things, events happen, journeys are taken, children are born, people die, there are conflicts and their resolutions.

- Third there is the first interpretive layer – where we see the obvious surface meaning of the story, the points that the original storyteller wanted to get across to her audience.

- Fourth there are deeper meanings, where we bring our own experiences and wisdom to bear on the story. Perhaps we compare two or three similar or connected stories. Here we find a message that we can learn from and apply today in our context or matrix. Here we will find general principles and broader ideas.

Let's get back to the steam train trip.

Some matrix

I'm just old enough to remember when steam trains were still in service on NZ railways in the late 1960s. The Christmas I was seven I was given a Triang model railway set and have enjoyed railways both full size and in model form ever since.

My Dad Paul remarried and moved to Brisbane in 1979 when I was 19. He has often come to visit and got to know his grandchildren in the years since then.

Second layer – A few details about our adventure

We went by ferry from Wellington to Picton, then by bus to Christchurch. The ferry ahead of us was late getting into Picton, where only one ferry can berth at a time, so our ferry soaked up the time by going around the top of Arapara Island instead of the usual route through Tory Channel.

We stayed with Heather's Mum Averil for two nights, before and after the steam train trip.

The railway between Christchurch and Greymouth is single track, with passing loops, where we had to wait for coal trains and regular passenger trains to pass us.

Because the Otira tunnel, down from Arthur's Pass to Otira, is very long and steep, and our carriages were older rolling stock, Kiwi Rail required us to disembark at Arthur's Pass and catch buses down to Otira for safety reasons.

Let's see some photos and video clips…

(For the four-minute short video on YouTube – see Links PDF at end.)

Third layer – some more obvious points.

Dad and I planned the trip and made bookings. But we had to rely on other people to help along the way. Sarah let me have a day off from the shop. The ferry crew, bus driver and Mainline Steam who ran the steam train, were professional and gave us safe, enjoyable journeys. Averil shared her home with us for two nights.

Unexpected events sometimes have silver linings. We saw a part of the Marlborough Sounds we had never seen before when the ferry captain made a detour.

When they announced on the train that we would have to transfer to buses at Arthur's Pass we were disappointed at first. But then it was pointed out to us that if we stayed in the train down through the Otira tunnel, all we would see was 15 minutes of darkness. Instead, we travelled on a dramatic, steep winding road, passed over the new Otira viaduct and saw bush and mountains we wouldn't have seen from the train.

On the train the seats were fixed, with two facing forward and two facing backwards and a table in between. So, we were face-to-face with strangers at the start of the journey. But we soon introduced ourselves and got to know each other. One of the men across the aisle had a birthday and his wife had packed a surprise birthday cake, which got cut up and passed around. By choosing to make new friends we had a more pleasant time.

Fourth layer – a bit deeper

Because Dad and I have lived physically so far apart for more than half my lifetime, we need to both be intentional about nurturing our relationship. I can't just pop down the road to see him. This trip was about having a shared experience and growing our relationship.

So, for relationships to succeed, we need to work at them.

On the steam trip getting to the destination was not the most important thing – the journey was. If Heather and I are driving somewhere, she is the one who wants to stop at a roadside stall to buy fruit or park and look at the view. I'm usually focussed on getting from point A to B in the shortest time.

On the steam trip I enjoyed the many photo stops and took lots of photos and video. The snowed covered mountains and the scenery were inspiring. I was thrilled to stop at Cass – we have a print in our lounge of Rita Angus' famous painting of Cass, and I was there. I felt the wind in my face when I went up to the open-air observation carriage.

So, I learned a little about enjoying the journey, being mindful and aware of the moment."

Back to the Bible (2023)

In the 2014 service I used the idea of multiple layers of meaning to explore: Exodus 32:1-14 – The Golden Calf, and Matthew 22:1-14 – The Parable of the Wedding Banquet.

A clearer example is Matthew 14:13-21: Feeding the Five Thousand.

Here are key lines from the NRSV text. The highlights are mine.

> …Jesus said to them, "They need not go away; **you give them something to eat.**" …**Taking** the five loaves and the two fish, he looked up to heaven and **blessed** and **broke** the loaves and **gave** them to the disciples, and the disciples gave them to the crowds.

Finding the layers of meaning

- **Matrix:** Jesus is journeying through Galilee ministering to the people who come to see him. The disciples journey with him. Under Herod Antipas' rule life is hard for people at the bottom of society and food is never plentiful.

- **Narrative level:** It is evening. The people who came to see Jesus are hungry. Jesus takes the five loves and two fish the disciples had with them, blesses the food and distributes it to the crowd. Everyone is fed well and there are 12 baskets of food left over.

- **A little deeper – trying to make sense of the story:** I used to believe that there were two possible ways to interpret this story. Either the story is factually correct, and Jesus miraculously created a surplus of food. Or the people all had some food with them which they kept hidden and only brought out and shared when they saw Jesus' example, i.e. they were in a sense shamed into sharing their food. Neither explanation appeals to me.

- **Deeper still:** Perhaps this story is really a parable; its meaning is symbolic. John Dominic Crossan draws attention to the words: **Took-Blessed-Broke-Gave**. What does this remind you of…? Yes, the last supper, the love feasts that the early house church Christians shared, and the Eucharist / Communion we participate in today in our churches.

- The story tells us that Eucharist / Communion is not a private act (as in the closed Upper Room) but an event to be held in the open to which all are invited.

This parable has a provocative edge, "…**you give them something to eat**" Jesus says to the disciples. We are challenged to do the same today.

Comments

- Short videos which you create can be a useful tool in worship. Less than 3 minutes is ideal.

- Most mobile phones today take excellent quality video. If you don't know how to edit a video to show in worship, ask your congregation for help. Someone will know what to do and will enjoy working with you.

- Do you find the idea that Bible stories have several layers of meaning useful?

- How could you apply this to the services you lead?

Learning

Our scriptures were written at least 2,000 years ago for people in a different time, place, society – matrix to us.

Showing how something from today, e.g. a train excursion, is related to a given story in the Bible will help your congregation to engage with and get new understandings of scripture.

Use your imagination…

33 – Railways as metaphors 3
– *This Ol' Freedom Train*

This chapter describes teaching the congregation the song *This Ol' Freedom Train* during a 2021 service themed around God's calling from 1 Samuel 3. The song, rooted in the history of the Underground Railroad, was sung unaccompanied in rounds, showing how congregations can create vibrant music with simple leadership. The key learning is that confident singers and repetition can draw people into participation, transforming a rough start into a joyful, united sound.

• • •

Introduction

Here's a song we taught the congregation during a service in the New Hall at our church on 17 January 2021, when we were using the hall for services while our historic church building was being earthquake strengthened.

We explored 1 Samuel 3:1-21 – Samuel's Calling – and my theme was *God's calling – Let's climb on board!*

The song talks about slaves in the southern United States in the 1800s making secret (Underground Railroad) journeys to the northern United States and Canada where they would be free.

See the Links PDF at the end for an MP3 sound file of the congregation singing led by Heather and Philip. The hall has a lively acoustic so the sound quality is not great – but you will get the idea of the song.

This Ol' Freedom Train
(Traditional)

This ol' Freedom Train
is such a long time in a'comin'
There ain't no one can't afford it,
So you'd better climb on board it.
Gimme that [clap] Free-ee-dom,
Gimme that [clap] Free-ee-dom,
Gimme that Freedom, Freedom, Freedom
Ch t ch, Ch t ch, Ch t ch, Ch

Learnings

Congregations can sing unaccompanied if they are led by confident singers.

For a round like this, the technique we use is to have everyone sing right through the song 2 or 3 times. Then we split the congregation into two groups (left and right) with one leader starting leading one group and the other leader starting a bar or two later leading the second group.

Notice how the round is a bit ragged at first, but as the congregation relax into the song and start to enjoy it, the sound improves.

I first learnt the song as a warm-up exercise for our Festival Singers choir rehearsals and added it to my worship *kete.*

> p.s. I displayed and talked about my model railway shunting layout before we sang the song. See chapter 34.

34 – Railways as metaphors 4
– Displaying a model railway

This chapter describes using a model railway shunting layout as a children's talk focus to illustrate the theme of God's call in the stories of Samuel and Jesus calling the disciples. The train imagery helped show how God continually adds people and resources for the journey of faith, with everyone invited to climb on board. The key learning is that sharing personal hobbies as props can create engaging, memorable connections between everyday life and scripture for both children and adults.

• • •

Introduction

For the Time with Children / Introducing the Theme section of our service on 17 January 2021 I displayed my model railway shunting layout and moved some coaches by hand as props as I talked.

Tip

I write out in full what I am going to say during the Time with Children. I then ad lib what I say in the service, confident that I will make the key points.

Here are the notes I wrote for this service:

"One of our Bible stories for today is about God calling Samuel in the night.

Samuel was a boy about 9 or 10 years old. He lived in the temple with the priest Eli. One night when he was sleeping, he woke up and heard a voice calling, "Samuel, Samuel." Samuel thought that Eli had called him, so he went to Eli's room and said, "here I am." And Eli said I didn't call you, go back to bed. This happened three times. After the third time Eli said to Samuel it must be God who is calling you. Next time you hear the call get up and say "Speak. I'm your servant, ready to listen." And that is what Samuel did, and God gave him a message about Eli's family.

Samuel grew up and became the most important priest and prophet of his time. And God kept calling Samuel and giving him messages about what was going to happen and what God wanted Samuel to do.

There are other stories about God calling people in the Old Testament. God called Noah to build an ark before the flood came. God called Moses to lead God's people out of Egypt. In the New Testament Jesus called Zacchaeus the tax collector to get down out of the tree and share a meal with Jesus.

The other Bible story today is about Jesus calling Philip to be a disciple. Then Philip called Nathanael to come and see Jesus, and Nathanael became a disciple too.

I think that God calling Samuel and Jesus calling Philip is like a guard calling passengers to climb on board a train. Our journey through life is like a train journey.

Came and have a close look at this model railway I have made. [Uncover shunting layout – say that adults may like to come and have a look too]

This passenger train only has one carriage. Is that going to be enough to carry all the people when God and Jesus have called? No. Let's add another carriage. ["Hand of God" adds rolling stock one at a time.] It isn't as nice as the first carriage, but it will do. Is that going to be enough? No let's add another carriage. And another. And we're going to need some food and supplies for our journey so let's add a couple of goods wagons of supplies. And we need a van for the guard. Maybe we need another engine to help climbing hills.

This rail car isn't ready to leave yet. And it might go in another direction. Its passengers haven't been called yet. And this loco is getting serviced in the loco shed ready for its next journey.

Let's check that the points are switched the right way. Are we ready to go? Yes. OK so now the signal drops to show the line ahead is clear and off we go.

At the end of their shift the engine driver and fireman will get off the train to rest. And a fresh, new driver and fireman will take their place.

Sometimes in our lives we will we want to get off the train and stay in one place for a while. When we feel called again and ready to move on, we can catch the next train."

We then sang *This Ol' Freedom Train* (see chapter 33).

Comments

Physical objects which people can hold, or even just look at, help them to engage with the message.

My portable layout is simple and leaves much for the imagination to fill in. But I like making the buildings from scratch and get pleasure from the hobby.

Both adults and children enjoyed coming forward out of their seats to look at the layout.

Learnings

Share with your congregation hobbies or crafts that you enjoy, e.g. wood turning crochet/knitting, pottery, painting, dance, book binding...

You will surprise yourself with the links you can make between your hobby and the scripture readings for the day.

I sit quietly for a few minutes, with my eyes shut, and wait for an idea to form...

People will appreciate learning more about you and will be more receptive to the messages you present to them.

(See also chapter 8)

General Ideas

35 – Building the Service Together

This chapter introduces a modular, participatory approach to worship where the congregation helps shape the liturgy in real time by selecting or creating prayers and other elements. By preparing multiple options in advance and inviting people to co-write intercessions or lead parts of the service, worship becomes collaborative rather than scripted. The result is a Spirit-led, shared act of creation that fosters ownership, inclusivity, and deeper engagement.

• • •

Introduction

This interactive worship format empowers your congregation to help build the liturgy – choosing elements and creating prayers in the moment – for a service that is truly shared.

The Idea

What if the congregation helped shape the service as it unfolded? What if, instead of following a fixed script, you created worship together – with participants choosing, composing, and offering different parts of the liturgy?

Building the Service Together is a modular approach to worship that hands creative responsibility back to the people. It invites spontaneity, prayerfulness, and a sense of shared ownership – without becoming chaotic or unstructured.

This is worship as collaboration, not performance.

How It Works

Prepare multiple options in advance

Before the service, select and print a range of choices for key parts of the liturgy. For example:

- 5 Calls to Worship
- 5 Opening Prayers
- 5 Prayer of Approach & Words of Assurance pairs

- 5 Offertory Prayers
- 5 Sending Forth / Benedictions

(See the Sample Prayers & Liturgy section later in this book)

Arrange these attractively on a table or pin board – clearly labelled and easy to read. You might colour-code them, laminate the cards, or display them on a screen if that suits your setting.

Invite volunteers to lead

As the service begins, explain the format and ask for volunteers:

> "This morning, we're building our worship together. Who would like to select our Call to Worship from the five on offer?"

You'll be surprised by how readily people step forward – especially once they realise, they don't need to write anything themselves.

Creating New Content Together

Not every part needs to be pre-written. Some elements can be co-created live.

Prayers of Intercession

Invite the congregation to help write a six-stanza prayer, using a simple format.

- Each stanza has four lines
- The same congregational response follows each one.

Organise people into small groups or individuals and assign them a stanza to write – perhaps one for each of these themes:

- The world
- Our country
- The Church
- Our community
- Those in need
- Those who have gone before us

Encourage one group to write the repeated congregational response. Allow a few minutes for quiet writing, with gentle music or silence.

When ready, invite each person or group to come forward and read their stanza aloud. The congregation responds after each one.

The result is a living, breathing expression of your community's shared prayers.

Tips for Success

- Keep the language accessible – avoid dense theology or jargon.
- Show the structure visually – project a basic Order of Service or print it out. Chapter 4 offers a helpful, well-tested model.
- Be flexible – allow space for reflection, silence, or improvisation.
- Use gentle background music during writing or choosing moments.
- Have a backup plan – keep one pre-written version of each element on hand in case no one volunteers.

Why this approach works

This style of service:

- Invites participation without pressure
- Makes space for the Spirit to move in the moment
- Models that *every member is a minister*
- Honours a diversity of voices and styles, and
- Builds ownership and deeper engagement.

Summary

When we build the service together, worship becomes more than something we attend – it becomes something we *create*, with God and with one another.

36 – Finding the Divine in the Everyday
– *God is in the Small Things*

This chapter presents my prayer *God is in the Small Things*, which celebrates God's presence in the ordinary details of daily life through vivid sensory imagery. It reminds us that small acts of connection, kindness, and awareness can reveal the sacred woven into both creation and human relationships. Worship leaders are encouraged to adapt and use the prayer in creative ways, helping congregations cultivate gratitude and mindfulness in everyday moments.

• • •

Introduction

The prayer *God is in the Small Things* – from my PDF eBook *Kindle A Flame* – offers a reminder that God's presence is not confined to grand gestures or extraordinary events but can be found in the seemingly insignificant moments of our daily lives.

This prayer invites us to awaken our senses and appreciate the divine spark that resides in the ordinary, fostering a deeper awareness of God's constant presence.

Here's the prayer…

God is in the small things

Lord, open our eyes to your creation:
A fiery sunset on a wide horizon
A spider's delicate web, spangled with dew
The vibrancy of a child's painting
The miniature world of life in a rock pool
You are in the small things that we *see* every day

Lord, open our ears to:
A tui's song
Children's laughter in the playground
Music of the city street and traffic's hum
The joy of a choir singing
You are in the small things that we *hear* every day

Lord, help us savour:
A meal prepared with love for us by another person
The tang of an exotic fruit
The morning's first cup of coffee or tea
An ice cream at the beach
You are in the small things that we *taste* every day

Lord, help us breathe in the smell of:
Salt spray on the wind
Dripping wet native bush on a walk
A newborn baby's head
Mahoe tree flowers on a still night
You are in the small things that we *smell* every day

Lord, help us to feel:
The warmth of a handshake or hug
A pat on the shoulder when we are sad
The softness of an animal's fur
The smoothness of a river pebble
You are in the small things that we *touch* every day

Lord help us as we:
Smile shyly at a new neighbour or classmate
Make a cuppa for a friend
Serve on a committee
Sing in a choir
You are in the small things that we *do* every day

Lord help us to wonder at:
Coming to church each week and leaving refreshed
Pohutukawa blossom at Christmas
Holding a child's hand as they walk to school
The Southern Cross on a clear night
Your love is in the small things that we keep in our hearts. Amen.

Key Themes: A Celebration of the Mundane

- **God's Presence in Creation:** The prayer emphasises God's presence throughout creation, highlighting the beauty and wonder found in both the natural and human-made world.
  From sunsets to spider webs, children's artwork to bustling city streets, God's handiwork is evident in the tapestry of our everyday experiences.

- **Awakening the Senses:** The prayer uses vivid sensory language to draw us into a deeper awareness of the world around us. It encourages us to truly see, hear, taste, smell, and touch the small things, fostering a sense of mindfulness and gratitude for the simple joys that often go unnoticed.

- **Finding the Sacred in the Ordinary:** The prayer challenges us to shift our perspective and recognise the sacredness inherent in the ordinary. By acknowledging God's presence in our daily routines and interactions, we elevate the mundane to the realm of the spiritual, transforming our perception of the world.

- **The Importance of Human Connection:** The prayer underscores the significance of human connection and the ways in which God's love is revealed through our relationships. Sharing a meal, offering a comforting touch, or simply smiling at a stranger are acts of love and kindness that reflect God's presence in our lives.

- **Small Acts of Faith:** The prayer highlights the profound impact of seemingly small acts of faith and service. Attending church, supporting a friend, or simply taking a moment to appreciate the beauty of the night sky are all ways in which we can nurture our relationship with God and contribute to the well-being of others.

Practical Applications for Worship Leaders

This prayer's simple message makes it a versatile tool for worship leaders seeking to create a more mindful and engaging worship experience. Here are several ways to effectively use *God is in the Small Things* during services:

- **Call to Worship:** Begin the service by reading the prayer aloud, inviting the congregation to enter a posture of attentiveness and gratitude for God's presence in their lives.

- **Responsive Reading:** Engage the congregation in a responsive reading of the prayer, with the leader reciting the first line of each stanza and the congregation responding with the affirmation **"You are in the small things..."** This approach encourages active participation and emphasises the shared experience of finding God in the everyday.

- **Visual Enhancements:** Project images that correspond to each stanza of the prayer, such as a sunset, a spider web, a cup of tea, or a child's hand. Visual aids can deepen the impact of the prayer and help the congregation connect with its message on a more sensory level.

- **Musical Accompaniment:** Consider incorporating soft instrumental music or ambient soundscapes that evoke the sounds of nature or everyday life during the reading of the prayer. This can enhance the contemplative atmosphere and encourage a sense of peace and reflection.

- **Personal Reflection:** Encourage the congregation to take a moment of silence after the prayer to reflect on their own experiences of finding God in the small things. This provides an opportunity for personal connection with the prayer's message and fosters a deeper understanding of its relevance to their lives.

Adapting the Prayer for Specific Contexts

The prayer's structure and themes lend themselves well to adaptation for specific contexts or liturgical seasons. For example, during Advent, the prayer could be modified to focus on finding God's presence amid busyness and preparation, while during Lent, it could emphasise the importance of simple acts of service and sacrifice.

You could personalise the prayer by substituting words and phrases that resonate with your local culture and environment. This ensures that the prayer remains relevant and meaningful for your congregation.

Extending the Message Beyond the Service

The message of *God is in the Small Things* can extend beyond the walls of the church and inspire a more mindful and grateful approach to everyday life. Encourage the congregation to carry the prayer's message with them throughout the week, actively seeking out God's presence in the ordinary moments of their daily routines.

By embracing the prayer's invitation to find God in the small things, we can cultivate a deeper awareness of God's constant love and presence, transforming our lives and our communities one small act of faith at a time.

37 – Rewriting a Parable in Modern Form Together

This chapter introduces a participatory practice of rewriting Jesus' parables in modern settings, helping congregations engage scripture with fresh relevance. By collaboratively re-imagining familiar stories like the Good Samaritan using today's contexts, people uncover new insights into compassion, justice, and neighbourliness. The activity fosters theological reflection in community, allowing the Spirit to speak through contemporary storytelling while honouring Jesus' original intent.

• • •

Introduction

This chapter gives you a fresh, participatory way to engage congregations with scripture – by collaboratively rewriting a familiar parable in language and imagery that speaks directly to today.

Parables were never meant to stay stuck in ancient Palestine. Jesus told stories using the images and issues of his time – robbers, roadways, religious roles – to provoke, confront, and illuminate. So why not continue his method?

One powerful, creative form of worship leadership is to invite your community to retell a parable in modern terms. You don't need to be a drama group or a professional writer. All you need is an openness to listen together, imagine, and reshape.

A great place to start is the story of the Good Samaritan (Luke 10:25-37). Most of us know the shape:

- Someone gets hurt
- People who should help walk by
- The least expected person stops, acts with compassion, and crosses boundaries of prejudice

But if you pause and look again, the parable is crying out to be re-imagined. The road from Jerusalem to Jericho might now be a motorway, a city alley, a border zone, or a corporate hallway.

Leading the activity

Here's how to lead the activity.

- Read the parable aloud – slowly and without commentary.
- Ask open-ended questions:
  - If Jesus told this story today, where might it take place?
  - Who would the modern-day priest and Levite be?
  - Who would be the unexpected hero?
  - What would "bandaged his wounds" look like now?
- Divide into small groups and invite each to brainstorm a version of the parable set in their community, city, or country. Encourage the use of everyday language and current events.
- Come back together and share each group's version. If possible, act one out or read as a dramatic monologue. Let the stories challenge, move, or discomfort – just like Jesus' parables did.

Here's a possible rewrite:

In the bustle of central Auckland, a young woman is suddenly attacked, robbed and left hurt and dazed sitting on the footpath. People stream past, busy with their own lives. A pastor wearing a clerical collar glances down at her phone and keeps walking. A politician notices the scene, but quickly crosses the street to avoid getting involved.

Then a homeless man pushing a shopping trolley filled with his worldly possessions comes along. He stops. Spotting a café nearby, he grabs their first aid kit, kneels beside her, and tends to her wounds as best he can. He waits with her until the ambulance arrives. Passers-by mock him, sneer at the sight of a man like him helping. Yet when she tells her story later, she simply says: "He was my neighbour."

Summary

This isn't just a novelty activity. It's theological reflection in community. It lets people step inside the parable, find themselves in the story, and listen for what the Spirit might be saying *now*.

When we rewrite the parables together, we honour Jesus' storytelling gift – and discover the radical grace still pulsing through his words.

38 – Winter Garden, Compost and Resurrection

This chapter uses the imagery of winter gardens and compost to illustrate how decay and rest are integral to the process of resurrection and spiritual renewal. It encourages worship leaders to embrace the slow, earthy transformation of winter through tactile rituals, altars, and biblical gardening metaphors. The message is that resurrection begins not only in spring but in the hidden, sacred work of winter's soil.

• • •

Introduction

Here is a grounded, seasonal metaphor for spiritual transformation, with practical ideas for winter-themed services.

In winter, my garden looks dead. The soil is cold. The plants have either been pruned back, pulled out, or have withered to brittle stalks. The compost heap steams quietly in the corner – not pretty, but alive with invisible transformation. And that, I believe, is the gospel in winter.

This season of hibernation and decay is not the opposite of resurrection. It is part of it. As we wait through winter and look ahead to spring's arrival in three months' time, we are offered a gift – the chance to re-imagine resurrection not as a dazzling moment, but as a deep, earthy process.

Think of compost. It begins with leftovers, scraps, dead things – banana peels, weeds, tea bags, grass clippings, leaves. All useless on their own. But given time, moisture, and warmth, they break down and become rich, fertile soil. Compost is slow resurrection. The old is transformed, not discarded. The dead feeds the living.

Embracing the metaphor

Worship in winter can embrace that earthy metaphor.

- What are the things in our spiritual lives that need to break down before new life can emerge?
- What failed plans, worn-out rituals, or tired theologies need to be surrendered to the soil?

Here are a couple of ideas to try in a service:

- Invite people to write down, on small sheets of paper, a phrase or idea that represents something they are ready to let go of. Place these on top of a bucket of compost you've brought from your garden. The paper will decompose and become part of the mix that supports new growth in spring.

- Try creating a "winter altar" in your sanctuary – sparse, earthy, and real. Place a bowl of compost at its centre. Add bare branches, rough cloth, and dirty garden gloves. Invite people to come forward and touch these objects. Let them reflect on what's hidden in their lives that is quietly changing.

- In your sermon, draw on biblical gardening metaphors that reflect this slow rhythm: seeds falling into the earth, vines being pruned, fig trees left barren for a season. Pair them with silence, tactile prayer, and reflective music.

The point is not to rush to spring. Let winter be winter. Honour the rest. Honour the rot and die-back. Remind your community that this too is resurrection. The steaming compost pile is already preparing the garden for new life. Resurrection doesn't begin only on Easter Sunday – it begins now, in the cold, dark ground.

Let the soil and the Spirit do their slow, sacred work.

Summary

Even in winter's stillness, God's transforming power is quietly at work – composting the old, nourishing the roots, and preparing the ground for resurrection.

39 – Circle the Story
– Movement-Based Worship for All Ages

This chapter introduces *Circle the Story*, a movement-based worship practice that uses circles and spirals to embody unity, journey, and belonging. By inviting congregations to gather, walk, dramatize stories, or pray in circular forms, worship becomes participatory and intergenerational. The practice highlights that faith is not only spoken but lived through shared movement, symbolising connection, equality, and the rhythm of God's love.

• • •

Introduction

Here is a gentle, low-barrier way to invite movement into worship – using circles, spirals, and physical space to embody themes of unity, journey, and belonging.

The Idea

Worship isn't just something we hear – it's something we do with our whole selves.

Circle the Story invites people to move together in sacred space, using the simple, ancient shape of the circle to reflect God's love, the journey of faith, and the rhythm of return.

No choreography required. Just a willingness to step out of the pews and move as a body – one community, one flow, one Spirit.

Why Circles?

The circle is a sacred symbol woven through creation: the sun, the moon, the rings of a tree, the ripple on water, the shared table. It speaks of unity, wholeness, and connection – and in worship, it reminds us we belong to something greater than ourselves.

Circles and spirals echo biblical movement:

- The Israelites circling Jericho
- The prodigal returning home
- Jesus teaching in a circle of friends

- The early church gathered around the bread and cup
- Circles have no hierarchy. No sharp corners. Everyone is equidistant from the centre.

How to Use Circle Movement in Worship

Here are four gentle, inclusive ways to incorporate circle-based movement into a service:

1. Gathering in a Circle

At the beginning or end of worship, invite the congregation to form a large circle (or multiple overlapping ones if needed). This can symbolise:

- Unity in diversity
- Our shared identity in Christ
- Equality and connection

Light a candle in the centre, sing a round, or pass a blessing hand-to-hand around the circle.

2. Walking the Spiral

Using chalk, string/rope, or small stones, create a spiral labyrinth in the worship space. During a quiet song or reflection time invite people to:

- Walk inward to pray, release, or listen
- Pause at the centre
- Walk outward, returning renewed

This simple ritual can follow a sermon or be used during a prayer time.

3. Dramatizing a Story in a Circle

Use the circle to embody a biblical story.

- In the parable of the lost sheep, one person steps out from the circle; a "shepherd" walks the perimeter to bring them home.
- In the Emmaus story, walk a spiral path as the narrative unfolds, reflecting the journey from grief to recognition.

These movements make the story real and memorable – especially for all-age worship.

4. Prayers in Motion

Invite the whole circle to join in simple shared gestures – placing hands over hearts, raising arms, or turning slowly in place.

If the people are comfortable to do this, ask them to turn 90 degrees and rest their left hand on the right shoulder of the person next to (in front of) them, to form a continuously joined circle. Ask them to remain connected while walking slowly round the circle. While moving have them bend their knees a little to dip down then stand tall again. Repeat this rotating movement for at least 30 seconds.

These small motions enrich collective prayer with embodied meaning.

Tips for Success

- Clearly explain what's happening and why – this helps people feel safe.

- Ensure accessibility – provide chairs around the circle for those who prefer to sit.

- Use soft music or chant to create atmosphere.

- Focus on meaning, not performance – gentle, slow, and simple is best.

- This is especially effective in intergenerational services where movement helps everyone engage.

Summary

Circles remind us we are connected. Spirals remind us we are journeying.

When we move together in worship – even gently – we enact the gospel not just with our mouths, but with our bodies.

We circle the story until it lives within us.

40 – Following your heart... *Let it be*

This chapter reflects on a Beatles-themed worship service inspired by the *Get Back* documentary, exploring faith through the song *Let It Be* and the emotions it stirred. It describes how visual props, music, and congregational affirmations were woven into the service, while also sharing the challenges of technical glitches and the lessons learned. The central message encourages worship leaders to draw on personal experiences as creative inspiration, embrace imperfections, and trust that authentic worship connects despite small setbacks.

• • •

Introduction

Heather and I watched Peter Jackson's three-part *Get Back* documentary about The Beatles in the Christmas / New Year break (2022-23). I found the documentary very moving and was surprised to find myself crying at the end.

I shared with the congregation why I think I reacted that way and explored metaphors relating to our faith that are suggested by the documentary.

Three sections of the service on 29 January 2023 focussed on The Beatles and the documentary:

- **Time with children / Introducing theme:** I displayed some of my Beatles LPs and intended to play the official video trailer to the documentary
- **Sermon:** *Let It Be*
- **Song after the sermon:** Heather and I sang *Let It Be* (Lennon/McCartney)

One of the key techniques for me of leading creative worship services is to be on the lookout for experiences, events, objects & resources that can be used as inspiration for a service. I had a particularly strong emotional response after watching the last of the three documentaries.

I knew immediately that I wanted to use the documentary content in a service. It took a couple of weeks to figure out how I was going to approach this.

What I did

To provide a visual element for the congregation I took with me the 13 key Beatles LPs from my collection and set them out on the sanctuary steps, during the Introduction to the Theme slot.

At the end of that slot, I intended to play through the church projectors and sound system, the official trailer for the documentary so that the congregation could get a feel for the band, their music and the 1969 setting.

I tested the projection and sound 30 minutes before the service started and all was well. But, although I plugged the laptop into the power socket, I forgot to turn the power socket switch on, and the laptop battery died just before I was going to start the service.

So we lost the PowerPoint slides for the hymns and, more importantly, I couldn't play the video on my laptop as planned.

Technical tips

- To get good sound quality easily, I plugged powered speakers into my laptop on the front pew and sat one of the church radio microphones next to the speakers. The sound from the microphone then played through the church sound system which is controlled at the back of the church.

- Bring to your service a backup on a USB stick of the PowerPoint slides and any videos of sound recordings you want to play during the service. That morning, I had the church's laptop also with me at the front pew. I took a few minutes to plug in the church laptop to the power and the projectors, and copy the PowerPoint from the USB stick, so we had the slides for the hymn texts.

- Don't try to do everything yourself. For our services, I also set up a live-stream, and either run the sound system for other worship leaders or test the levels and that microphones are working correctly before starting my services. I also needed to ask someone to light the candles. Because of attending to these other things, I forgot to switch on the power for the laptop that would run the video. If you can, get someone else to help with audio visuals when you are leading a service, or at the least get someone to look over your shoulder to make sure you haven't forgotten anything.

- I played the video in the hall when we were having morning tea after the service. People enjoyed watching the trailer. It brought back memories for some of them. It would have been better if the video could have been played as intended in the service – oh, well…

Further connections with the theme

At the end of the sermon, I was inspired to try something I had not done before. *Amen* means *Let it be* or *Let it be so*. To a series of 9 affirmations, I asked the congregation to respond: "**And we say Amen, Let It Be.**"

Heather is a better guitarist than me and usually plays guitar when we want to sing a song for the congregation. This time I played and led the singing, with Heather in a supporting role. The song *Let It Be* works well in root position on guitar with finger picking runs between chords.

I challenged myself to get out of my comfort zone and play guitar. The song went OK.

For you to ponder…

Is there something you have had a strong emotional response to? Especially something that unexpectedly makes you joyful or sad or angry or hopeful.

Does your emotional response suggest a theme or idea to explore in your next service? Don't worry about whether your idea fits with the lectionary bible readings for the day.

Write down your ideas, then look at the lectionary readings. You will be surprised how easily a phrase or sentence in the bible reading pops out at you and meshes with your new theme.

A secret

I have never led a perfect service.

I always prepare well and try to foresee how the service will run. But there's often a small technical hitch, or I stumble over some words in the sermon, or…

The congregation will understand and not be worried. We are all just people gathering to worship God.

Links

See the Links PDF at the end for:

- The video trailer for the *Get Back* documentary about The Beatles.
- Readings and Sermon – Audio recording
- Whole Service – Audio recording
- Order of Service (Leader's version) – PDF

41 – Two Christmas Offerings

This chapter shares two creative resources for Advent worship: a simple round, *Christmas Hallelujah*, and a poem, *Christmas is Ours Again*. The round invites the congregation to sing in parts,, and symbolises the ongoing work of the Christmas message. Recordings and files are provided for learning. The poem reclaims the Nativity's meaning, encouraging a focus on love, hope, peace, and joy rather than consumerism.

• • •

About the round

Christmas Hallelujah

Halleluia, Christmas is coming.
Oh, let us praise the Lord.
Sing halleluia, welcome the Christ child,
Bringing hope for a peaceful world.

Christmas Halleluia

Sing as a round in 2 parts

Words & Music: Philip Garside

Hal - le - lu - ia, Christ - mas is com - ing. Oh, let us praise the Lord. Sing

hal - le - lu - ia, wel - come the Christ child, Bring - ing hope for a peace - ful world.

Sing unaccompanied.

The round works well in 2 or 4 parts. Start every two bars as indicated by the *.

I suggest that each part sings the melody 4 times through.

After teaching them the melody, you could ask one side of the congregation to start and then lead the other side of the congregation singing the second part.

The tune does not resolve in the last bar. For me this symbolises that the work of the Christmas message never ends.

Downloads to help you learn the round

See the Links PDF at the end for:

- A midi file of the melody – once through single part
- A midi file of the melody – four times through in two parts
- A midi file of the melody – four times through in four parts
- An MP3 file of the melody – once through single part
- An MP3 file of the melody – four times through in two parts
- An MP3 file of the melody – four times through in four parts
- Noteworthy Composer (2.75) setting
- An audio recording of our choir Festival Singers rehearsing the round in 4 parts.

About the poem

This poem is an attempt to reclaim the power of the Nativity stories and to shift our focus at Christmas away from commerce to things that have lasting value.

Christmas is Ours Again

Soft fall tears of joy
Down the face of the father
Smile now little boy
Warmed by your wondering mother
Love, hope, peace, joy
Christmas is ours again

Bright star, clear nights
Seen from far away
Journey in faith, no room for doubt
Kings bow to majesty
Love, hope, peace, joy
Christmas is ours again

You, me, what do we say
Can an old story still move us?
Offer wise gifts with open hearts
Treasure the laughter and song
Love, hope, peace, joy
Christmas is ours again.

44 – Re-imagining the *Lord's Prayer*

Discover a fresh way to engage with the *Lord's Prayer* by re-imagining its timeless words in today's language. This participatory worship activity invites congregations to explore the prayer's meaning in a contemporary context, deepening faith and connection. Ideal for churches seeking to blend tradition with creativity in meaningful, inclusive worship.

• • •

Why Re-imagine?

The *Lord's Prayer* is one of the most familiar and beloved prayers in the Christian tradition. Its rhythms and cadences have been spoken for generations in countless languages. For many, these words are deeply comforting.

Yet sometimes familiarity can dull our ears. We risk reciting the prayer by rote, without pausing to consider its meaning.

Re-imagining the *Lord's Prayer* together in fresh, contemporary language can awaken our hearts again. It invites us to listen with new ears, and to ask questions such as:

- What does "daily bread" mean in our community today?
- What does it mean to describe God as our parent?
- What does God's kingdom look like here and now?

This exercise is not about discarding the old words, but about rediscovering them.

It's creative, participatory, and open to people of different ages and stages of faith. By rewriting the prayer in our own voice, we learn to engage more deeply with its message.

Preparation

This activity works best in settings where people can talk together in smaller groups – such as café church gatherings around tables, or by creating circles of chairs in your usual worship space.

Practical steps:

- Provide large sheets of paper and markers or pens for each group.
- Have a large whiteboard or computer linked to a projector and screen at the front to collect the groups' ideas.
- Print copies of the version of the *Lord's Prayer* your church usually prays, for reference.

During the Service

Introduction
Begin by grounding the congregation in the significance of the prayer. You might say:

> "This is the prayer Jesus gave his disciples when they asked him how to pray. It speaks of trust, forgiveness, daily needs, and God's reign of love. Today we are going to listen with fresh ears and rewrite these words together in our own language for our own community."

Allow 20-30 minutes for the exercise. It could take the place of the sermon.

Action
- Read aloud your church's usual form of the prayer.
- Distribute copies, setting it out in one- or two-line sections, like this:

  > Our Father in heaven,
  > hallowed be your name,
  >
  > Your kingdom come, your will be done,
  > on earth as in heaven.
  >
  > Give us today our daily bread.
  >
  > Forgive us our sins
  > as we forgive those who sin against us.
  >
  > Lead us not into temptation
  > but deliver us from evil.
  >
  > For the kingdom, the power, and the glory
  > are yours now and forever. Amen.

- Assign each group one section (or the standalone line: *Give us today our daily bread*).
- Invite them to discuss what that section means today, then draft new words that capture the meanings and messages they uncover.

- Encourage plain, everyday language – words a child, neighbour, or newcomer to faith would understand.

Collaborative Draft

- When the groups are ready, invite them, in order, to share their rewritten lines.
- Record their new wording on the whiteboard or computer/projector screen for all to see.
- As each section is added, the congregation will see a new, parallel version of the *Lord's Prayer* take shape – their own collaborative version of Jesus' words.

Sharing the Prayer

Pray the new version aloud together for the first time.

Consider using it again later in the service – perhaps after communion, or as the final blessing.

Take a photo of the whiteboard and share it in the church newsletter or on social media.

If the new text resonates with your community, use it again in future worship services.

Closing Reflection

Conclude with words like these:

> "The prayer Jesus taught us is a gift for every generation. Today we have re-imagined it in words that speak to our hearts, our needs, and our community. May this remind us that prayer is not only about repeating sacred words – it is about bringing our lives honestly before God."

Why It Matters

Re-imagining the Lord's Prayer does more than refresh familiar language. It:

- Invites worshippers to own their faith in the present tense.
- Connects scripture with the daily struggles and hopes of your community.
- Bridges tradition and creativity, honouring both.
- Reminds us that prayer is a living conversation with God.

Done with care, this exercise can deepen trust, broaden understanding, and energise your congregation's shared spiritual life.

Prayers, Liturgy & Children's Talks

Introduction to
Prayers, Liturgy & Children's Talks

This section provides worship leaders with ten examples of each of these types of prayer or liturgy to adapt and use in your services:

- Calls to Worship
- Lighting the Candle
- Opening Prayers
- Prayers of Approach & Words of Assurance
- Prayers of Intercession
- Offering and Blessing of Offering
- Benediction / Sending Forth

I also provide ten sets of suggestions for activities for the Children's Talk / Introducing the Theme section of services.

All this material first appeared in my *Worship at Hand* weekly resource. While they were written for the Sundays noted, most of the prayers and ideas should also be suitable to use in your regular services.

The prayers are all responsive to encourage the congregation to engage with them.

I have not added "Amen" to the end of these prayers. Please do so as you consider appropriate.

45 – Calls to Worship

Come, people of God, from places of certainty and confusion,
We come with open hearts and questioning minds.

Jesus calls to us across the waters and down the road,
Offering new ways, new truth, new life.

When we are blinded by fear or belief,
God meets us with grace and a new vision.

When we think we've failed too deeply,
Christ feeds us, forgives us, and calls us again.

Let us gather to listen, to learn, and to follow,
For God is not finished with us yet.

Come, let us worship the living Christ.
We come to be transformed.

Easter 3 | Year C

Come, all who seek the risen Christ!
We come to honour lives of grace and courage.

Come, as Tabitha did, to offer your hands and heart.
We come, bringing acts of love and faith.

Come, like the widows, with your grief and hope held together.
We come with tears and thanksgiving.

Come, like Peter, to trust in the Spirit's power.
We come, ready to believe in what is possible.

In the name of Christ, life is restored, and love is renewed.
In this sacred gathering, we are made whole again.

Easter 4 | Year C

May God be gracious to us and bless us.
May God's face shine upon us.

Let every nation know the saving power of God.
Let all peoples praise the Holy One.

The earth yields its harvest, and justice springs forth.
God's abundance flows to every land.

Let the poor be lifted and the forgotten embraced.
Let all creation rejoice in God's care.

Come, people of God, gather in joy and truth.
We come to worship the One who blesses and sends.

Easter 6 | Year C

Come, people of God, clothed in Christ's mercy.
We gather as one body, stitched together in grace.

There is no longer Jew or Greek.
In Christ, we are one people.

There is no longer slave or free.
In Christ, we are made whole.

There is no longer male and female.
In Christ, we are set free to love.

From tombs of fear and fields of division,
God calls us into life abundant.

Come, and worship the One who clothes us in compassion.
We come to be made new in Christ.

Pentecost 2 | Year C

Come, all who seek healing and wholeness.
We come, trusting in God's power to restore.

Come, all who carry burdens too heavy alone.
We come, ready to share our struggles and hopes.

Come, those sent in Christ's name to proclaim peace.
We come, ready to say yes to the Spirit's call.

Come, those who have known rejection
and those who have known joy.
We come, with open hearts and resilient faith.

Come, through the wisdom of the young
and the courage of the humble.
We come, expecting God's power in simple acts.

In this time of worship, may the Spirit move among us.
We come, ready to receive and to be sent.

Pentecost 4 | Year C

God is near, not far off.
We gather to pray with open hearts.

Jesus teaches us how to reach toward the Holy.
We listen for the rhythm of sacred breath.

Not with many words, but with faithful longing,
We seek God's way in silence and speech.

In asking and knocking, in trusting and trying,
We come again to the Source of all life.

The One who gives bread, not stone,
Welcomes us with compassion and care.

Let us worship with courage and hope.
Let us worship the One who answers love with love.

Pentecost 7 | Year C

Set your minds on things above, where Christ is.
We lift our hearts to seek the things of heaven.

Put away the old self, with its anger and greed.
We come to be clothed in compassion and kindness.

Jesus warns us not to store up treasures for ourselves.
We seek to be rich toward God, not ourselves.

In Christ, there is no division, only beloved community.
We come together as one people, loved and renewed.

Let us worship the God who calls us to new life.
We gather with open hearts, ready to be transformed.

Pentecost 8 | Year C

Come, you who seek something unshakable
We come to the God whose voice still speaks

Not to fire and smoke, but to presence and peace
We come to Mount Zion, the city of grace

Come, you who long for meaning beyond the rules
We come to worship the One who heals on the Sabbath

Not in trembling fear, but in reverent awe
We come to the mediator of the new covenant

Let gratitude rise in this sacred gathering
Let awe awaken us to God's presence here

The Kingdom cannot be shaken
Let us worship with joy, freedom, and love.

Pentecost 11 | Year C

Come, all who long to live with depth and integrity
We gather to follow the One who leads us below the surface

Come, those stirred by ocean winds and sacred stories
We come to listen for God in water, word, and witness

Come, you who are ready to risk the cost of compassion
We come to walk with Christ, wherever he leads

Come, with aching questions and tender hope
We come, trusting that love can transform all things

Come, not for comfort, but for courage
We come to be reshaped by the call of discipleship

Come, with hearts open to truth, even when it disrupts
We come to learn the way of Christ, not convenience

Come, with reverence for creation and one another
We come to honour the sacred web that holds us all

Come, to the shore of a deeper gospel
We come, seeking the Spirit in the currents of grace

Come, for the world is breaking and being born again
We come to worship the God of costly love and wide mercy

Come, beloved of God, and dive into the holy unknown
We come, ready to be changed.

Pentecost 13 | Year C

Do not fret over those who seem to thrive through injustice
We gather to trust in the One who makes all things right

Let go of envy and lean into mercy
We come to rest in the promise of divine peace

Delight in the Holy One who plants joy in our souls
We seek not applause, but delight in God's love

Commit your path to God and let your trust be enough
We bring our questions, our hopes, our honest selves

Be still, and wait with holy patience
We pause to listen for the whisper of grace

Do not let anger rule or bitterness take root
We gather to be grounded in faith, not fear

Worship not outcomes, but presence
We come to be shaped by God's timing and truth

Put your trust in the God of quiet justice
We come, with mustard seeds of faith, to worship.

Pentecost 17 | Year C

46 – Lighting the Candle

In the blaze of divine encounter,
In the hush of hesitant trust,
A light shines on the road to change.

God speaks through fear, through vision, through love.
We light this flame for the courage to follow
And the grace to begin again.

Easter 3 | Year C

Light of mercy, flickering through mourning,
Flame of hope, kindled in the upper room,

Shine through every act of kindness,
Glow in lives stitched with compassion,

Burn in the courage to believe again,
Flare with the promise: life shall rise.

Easter 4 | Year C

We light this candle for vision and response,
For dreams that lead us beyond what is safe.

We light it for Lydia, bold and generous,
For the Spirit who opens hearts and homes.

We light it for journeys taken in trust.
May its flame guide us into welcome and grace.

Easter 6 | Year C

We light this candle
for the One who frees the bound,

for the One who clothes the shamed,
for the One who gathers the scattered,

for the One who restores the wounded,
for the One who makes us one.

Pentecost 2 | Year C

We light this candle
for the humble voices that speak wisdom.

We light this candle
for those who offer healing through simple acts.

We light this candle
for the Spirit who sends and sustains us.

Pentecost 4 | Year C

We light this candle for the Christ who dwells in us,
the fullness of God in a fragile body.

We light it for the Way we walk daily,
rooted in grace, shaped by love.

Let it shine in all our questions,
and call us again to the truth of who we are.

Pentecost 7 | Year C

We light this candle for the new life Christ brings.
In a world of greed and fear, light still shines.

It flickers in acts of kindness and truth.
It burns in our longing for justice and grace.

This flame reminds us we are hidden with Christ in God.
And we are called to shine with that same light.

Pentecost 8 | Year C

We light this candle for compassion that heals
For voices that speak mercy, not delay

For the One who saw a bent woman and set her free
For the Kingdom that cannot be shaken

For courage to stand tall in grace
For every soul God calls by name.

Pentecost 11 | Year C

We light this candle
for Christ, who speaks the hard word in love,

who walks with the Onesimuses of our day,
who disturbs the calm when truth must rise,

who calls us into deeper waters,
and whose flame reveals what lies beneath.

Pentecost 13 | Year C

We light this candle
for faith that begins small but grows bold.

For those who serve unseen and love without reward.
For the quiet courage to begin before we feel ready.

For the grace that does not count or compare.
For the flame of humble service that still lights the world.

Pentecost 17 | Year C

47 – Opening Prayers

God of road and shoreline,
Meet us in our places of doubt and discovery.

When we resist your leading,
Shine a light that we cannot ignore.

When we feel like failures,
Feed us with grace and call us again.

Teach us to trust your voice in unexpected places,
And follow you with courage and love.

Easter 3 | Year C

God of life, you breathe hope into sorrow,
And call us to believe beyond what we see.

You honour faith not just spoken, but lived,
In hands that serve, in hearts that give.

You come close to the grieving and the forgotten,
Bringing light into rooms filled with loss.

Revive our spirits, awaken our compassion,
Raise us, too, into lives of healing grace.

Easter 4 | Year C

God of healing and wholeness, you meet us where we lie.
You speak life into places we thought were dead.

In our waiting and our worry, you come close.
You see us, know us, and invite us to rise.

When despair holds us down, your grace lifts us up.
When rules restrict, your love breaks through.

Move among us now, O Christ.
Call us again to get up and walk.

Easter 6 | Year C

Gracious God, you clothe us with mercy.
We are covered in your love.

You cross boundaries to heal and welcome.
We are gathered by your grace.

You erase the lines that divide.
We are united in your Spirit.

You give us courage to tell our stories.
We will live as signs of your kingdom.

Pentecost 2 | Year C

Holy One, source of healing and hope,
We gather to listen and to learn.

Speak through the voices we least expect,
And guide us in humble service.

Open our hearts to your transforming Spirit,
And strengthen us for the journey ahead.

In simple acts and faithful steps,
We seek to embody your grace and peace.

Pentecost 4 | Year C

Christ, you are the ground beneath our feet.
Root us again in your life and love.

When distraction pulls us away,
Draw us back to what truly matters.

In your fullness, you dwell with us still.
Give us hearts to welcome your presence.

In all our thinking, speaking, and acting,
Let your grace take root and grow.

Pentecost 7 | Year C

Holy God, you invite us to seek what is above.
Set our hearts on your grace.

You call us to shed the burdens of the past.
Renew us with your Spirit.

You challenge the ways we store up and protect.
Free us from the fear that traps us.

You clothe us with a new identity in Christ.
Make us one, beloved and transformed.

Pentecost 8 | Year C

We come with open hands and hopeful hearts
We offer ourselves in reverence and awe

We come not to tremble, but to trust
We offer our praise with courage and joy

We come seeking grace, not perfection
We offer our lives in honest worship

We come to the unshakable Kingdom of God
We offer our thanks with all that we are.

Pentecost 11 | Year C

Holy God, you call us into costly grace
We come, needing courage to respond

You teach us to love beyond social lines
We come, needing hearts wide enough to follow

You unsettle what is easy and familiar
We come, needing vision beyond our comfort

You name the sacred in the exploited and erased
We come, needing faith to act with justice

You ask us to count the cost and carry the cross
We come, needing strength to keep going

You awaken hope in deep and hidden places
We come, needing joy that does not pretend

You are present where truth and love collide
We come, needing to be reshaped by your Spirit.

Pentecost 13 | Year C

O God of quiet strength and fierce compassion,
You teach us to trust, even when the world is loud.

We bring our envy, our weariness, our striving
And you invite us into stillness and joy

You call us to do good, not for reward
But because love is who we are

You root us in the long vision of justice
We turn again to your way, your grace, your peace.

Pentecost 17 | Year C

48 – Prayers of Approach & Words of Assurance

Gracious God, we come with questions and convictions,
Searching for truth, longing for peace.

Sometimes we are Saul – so sure we are right,
Until your light stops us in our tracks.

Sometimes we are Peter – ashamed, uncertain,
Until you call us back to love again.

In our blindness, bring clarity.
In our emptiness, bring abundance.

When we grow weary, renew our strength.
When we feel unworthy, remind us of your grace.

Meet us here, transforming Christ,
And make this time holy.

Words of Assurance

Even in our worst moments, Christ still comes to us.
Even when we resist or run away, God's grace finds us.
We are not disqualified by doubt or failure.
We are loved, called, and sent once more.

Easter 3 | Year C

Holy Shepherd, you walk with us through questions and storms,
You know us by name and call us to follow.

In a world that doubts and divides,
You remain our steady voice, clear and true.

Though others may not believe or understand,
We listen for your whisper and walk in your way.

You hold our lives in the safety of your hand,
And no one can snatch us from your love.

We come with hearts open,
To be led again by your grace.

You and the Creator are one,
And we are your people, forever embraced.

Words of Assurance

You are known by the One who calls your name.
You are held in the hand of the Shepherd.
No fear, no failure, no power can pull you away from God's love.
You are safe, chosen, and cherished.

Easter 4 | Year C

Loving God, you call to us in dreams and in silence.
We come, listening for your voice.

You find us beside pools of despair and rivers of hope.
You see us, even when we feel unseen.

You stir our hearts like Lydia's and invite us to rise
like the man on the mat.
In your mercy, give us courage to respond.

Strip away our excuses and awaken our longing.
Unblock what is stuck; unfreeze what is afraid.

Gather us into your story once more.
With faith renewed, we step toward you.

Here we are, God of grace.
Welcome us in, and lead us out.

Words of Assurance

Christ sees us in our waiting, our weariness, and our wanting.
He does not ask us to earn grace, only to receive it.
In every broken moment, healing is already moving toward us.
Get up. Walk in newness and freedom.

Easter 6 | Year C

Holy One, you know the fears that bind us.
Free us for love.

You see the barriers we build.
Break them down with grace.

You hear the voices we silence.
Restore our hearing and our hearts.

You meet us among the tombs and in the marketplaces.
You clothe us in hope and send us to speak.

Gather us close today.
Knit us together in Christ.

Set a fire of compassion in us.
Send us into the world to be healers.

Be the centre of our worship and our lives.
In you, we find our name and our home.

Words of Assurance

In Christ, we are clothed with compassion.
In Christ, we are healed from shame.
In Christ, we are called beloved.
No tomb, no chain, no past defines us.

Pentecost 2 | Year C

God of healing rivers and dusty roads,
We return to you in worship.

When pride blinds us to simple solutions,
Humble us with your wisdom.

When fear holds us back from your calling,
Fill us with resilient courage.

When we doubt our worth or ability,
Remind us that you empower the willing.

In our gathering, may burdens be lifted,
And your peace rest upon us.

In our sending, may we carry grace outward,
And walk as bearers of your healing love.

Words of Assurance

Even when we resist, God's grace remains steadfast.
Through humility and trust, healing flows anew.
God calls us beloved and equips us for the journey.
We are forgiven, restored, and renewed.

Pentecost 4 | Year C

We come to you again, O God,
knocking on the door of your presence.

Our hearts are noisy, our lives are full,
but still we long for quiet and connection.

Teach us to pray, not for answers only,
but for courage, trust, and inner peace.

Let your name be holy in our lives,
in our choices, our speaking, our silence.

Let your reign come near – in us,
and through us, in this hurting world.

Give us today what we truly need,
and help us to release what we cannot hold.

Forgive our forgetting, and help us to forgive,
as you shape us again into your likeness.

Words of Assurance

In Christ, the fullness of God's love has already been given.
We are not condemned but made alive with grace.
Our old burdens are nailed to the cross,
and we are raised to walk in freedom.

Pentecost 7 | Year C

We come, O God, not with riches but with longing.
We are here because we need you.

We confess the clutter of our lives and our minds.
We are here to make space for your truth.

We have dressed ourselves in fear, in anger, in pride.
We are here to be clothed anew.

You remind us that life is more than possessions.
We are here to live generously.

You call us not to hoard, but to share.
We are here to build your kingdom.

You tell us Christ is our life, hidden and revealed.
We are here to find that life again.

Words of Assurance

God has already clothed us in mercy and grace.
We are forgiven, renewed, and made one in Christ.
The treasures of love and justice are already ours.
We are set free to live a new life.

Pentecost 8 | Year C

God of wholeness, we come bent by burdens
Lift us with your gentle hand

We are tangled in old rules and rigid fears
Call us into freedom with your voice of grace

We have seen suffering, and sometimes turned away
Touch us with your compassion, and change us

We want to walk in your Way, not just know it
Open us to your living truth

We bring our distractions, our doubts, our weariness
We lay them down at your feet

Let this be our place of healing
Let this be our moment to stand tall again

In your presence, we find our truest home
In your mercy, we are made whole.

Words of Assurance

You have come not to fear, but to the city of the living God.
You are held in grace, not condemned by rules.
Through Jesus, the mediator of the new covenant, you are set free.
Nothing can shake the love that claims you.

Pentecost 11 | Year C

Jesus, you ask more of us than we often dare
Draw us beyond shallow faith

You disrupt comfort with compassion
Draw us beyond shallow faith

You refuse to ignore the value of the voiceless
Draw us beyond shallow faith

You lift the hidden burdens of the exploited
Draw us beyond shallow faith

You call us to reorder everything
Draw us beyond shallow faith

We bring our distractions, our defensiveness, our doubts
Draw us beyond shallow faith

We bring our longing to live with depth and meaning
Draw us beyond shallow faith

We are here to worship, not to escape
Draw us beyond shallow faith

We are here to be changed, not merely comforted
Draw us beyond shallow faith

We are here to honour the *va* – the sacred space between all things
Draw us beyond shallow faith

We release the fear of losing what is unjust
Draw us beyond shallow faith

We open ourselves to the fierce gentleness of your way
Draw us beyond shallow faith.

Words of Assurance

Even where systems enslave and discipleship costs,
Christ meets us with unmeasured mercy.
You are not alone, and you are not beyond grace.
You are beloved, forgiven, and called.

Pentecost 13 | Year C

We come with trembling faith and tangled thoughts
We come just as we are, and that is enough

We bring doubts that sit beside our hope
We bring hearts both bruised and brave

We come not seeking applause
But to walk quietly in your way

Teach us to serve without entitlement
To trust without needing all the answers

You call us to begin before we feel ready
So here we are, mustard seeds and all

We confess how often we measure worth by outcome
But you delight in presence, not performance

We name our longing to be seen and affirmed
But you invite us to find joy in simple faithfulness

We admit how fear keeps us from loving boldly
Yet your Spirit stirs in us a deeper courage

We return to the truth that grace does not compete
And in your presence, we are already enough.

Words of Assurance

You do not need perfect faith to be perfectly loved.
God delights in your questions as well as your trust.
In Christ, grace does not tally or measure.
You are held, forgiven, and free.

Pentecost 17 | Year C

49 – Prayers of Intercession

For the peoples of the world, and all who seek peace:
O Christ, who meets us on every road,
guide the nations into mercy and justice.
Break down walls of violence and fear.
Bring reconciliation where there is division.
Christ, transform and restore.

For our country, our leaders, and all who serve the common good:
Open hearts and minds to wisdom beyond politics.
May vision and courage shape every decision.
Lead us in pathways of compassion and equity.
Christ, transform and restore.

For your church in every land, and for our congregation:
Where faith feels tired or uncertain, renew our hope.
Where churches resist change, break open new beginnings.
Feed us again with your love and send us out with joy.
Christ, transform and restore.

For our local community and all who work for its well-being:
Bless schools, hospitals, and neighbourhood initiatives.
Help us listen to each other with respect and care.
May this place become more just, more welcoming, more kind.
Christ, transform and restore.

For all who are suffering, sick, grieving, or afraid:
We silently name those known to us…
Bring your comfort, healing, and peace.
Surround them with your presence and our love.
Christ, transform and restore.

For those who have died, and for our hope beyond the grave:
We remember those we love who are now with you.
Hold our grief gently and remind us of resurrection.
Keep us faithful until we feast with all the saints.
Christ, transform and restore.

Easter 3 | Year C

God of life and compassion, we pray for the world and its people.
Christ our Shepherd, guide us with love.

For nations in conflict and communities torn by violence,
Bring resurrection where death reigns and peace where fear grows.
Christ our Shepherd, guide us with love.

For Aotearoa New Zealand and all who lead us,
Give wisdom shaped by justice and courage rooted in compassion.
Christ our Shepherd, guide us with love.

For your Church in all places and traditions,
Revive us to be communities of healing, hope, and hospitality.
Christ our Shepherd, guide us with love.

For our local communities, neighbours, and families,
Teach us to walk alongside the hurting and lift up the weary.
Christ our Shepherd, guide us with love.

For those who are sick, suffering, grieving, or forgotten,
Raise them up with love as you raised Tabitha with hope.
Christ our Shepherd, guide us with love.

For all who have gone before us in faith and love,
May their legacy of kindness be our light, and their memory a blessing.
Christ our Shepherd, guide us with love.

Easter 4 | Year C

God of all nations, stir hearts and leaders toward peace.
May visions of justice replace dreams of domination.
We pray for countries in conflict, and for the courageous peacemakers.
Lord, in your mercy, hear our prayer.

Bless Aotearoa with wisdom, integrity, and compassion.
Guide all who govern, legislate, and lead communities.
Let their decisions uplift the vulnerable and serve the common good.
Lord, in your mercy, hear our prayer.

Like Lydia, may we open our hearts and homes to your Spirit.
Strengthen ministers, lay leaders, and congregations
with faith and grace.
Make your church a place of welcome, healing, and justice.
Lord, in your mercy, hear our prayer.

Shine your blessing over neighbourhoods, schools, and workplaces.
Bring renewal where there is weariness, and hope where there is hurt.
Help us walk beside the overlooked and uplift the weary.
Lord, in your mercy, hear our prayer.

We remember those paralysed by pain, grief, or despair.
May your words of life stir them to rise again.
Surround them with kindness, and grant strength for each new day.
Lord, in your mercy, hear our prayer.

We give thanks for saints and ancestors,
for faithful companions now at rest.
In their memory, may we live boldly and love generously.
Bring us all, in time, to your river of joy and your healing grace.
Lord, in your mercy, hear our prayer.

Easter 6 | Year C

For the peoples of the world:
Where division leads to war, and difference becomes reason for hate,
May your justice rise like the dawn and your mercy like the tide.
Clothe the nations in compassion, and break the chains of fear.
Christ, clothe us in your peace.

For our country and its leaders:
When self-interest overshadows wisdom
and the loudest voices drown the true,
Raise up leaders with humility and hearts tuned to the common good.
Let inclusion be policy and grace be practice.
Christ, clothe us in your peace.

For the church, here and everywhere:
When we are tempted to build walls or enforce old divisions,
Remind us we are one body, clothed in Christ and called to love.
May our worship and witness be signs of your unity.
Christ, clothe us in your peace.

For our local communities:
Where neighbours are strangers and isolation grows,
Plant seeds of connection, and let healing take root
in small kindnesses.
Restore our streets and schools, homes and hopes.
Christ, clothe us in your peace.

For those who suffer, are sick, or in need:
For the shamed and silenced, the burdened and broken,
the unwell and unwanted,
Bring wholeness that honours dignity and love that casts out fear.
Let each soul be seen, and none be left out.
Christ, clothe us in your peace.

For those who have died, and for our hope in you:
Hold those we remember in the light of your eternal presence.
Comfort all who mourn with the promise of your risen life.
We give thanks for the saints, and for the story you are still writing.
Christ, clothe us in your peace.

Pentecost 2 | Year C

For the peoples of the world:
God of all nations, where pride breeds division
and power wounds the vulnerable,
Raise up peacemakers and healers who cross boundaries.
God of simple acts, hear our prayer.

For our country and its leaders:
Guide those in authority to choose compassion over self-interest,
And to listen to the wisdom of the unheard and unseen.
God of simple acts, hear our prayer.

For our church and its leaders:
Bless our churches with the courage to serve humbly,
To proclaim your peace boldly, and to seek the Spirit's leading.
God of simple acts, hear our prayer.

For our local communities:
In places of struggle, isolation, or injustice,
Help us share resources, build resilience, and offer hope.
God of simple acts, hear our prayer.

For those who are suffering, sick, or in need:
Bring healing to bodies, minds, and spirits;
Surround carers and families with strength and compassion.
God of simple acts, hear our prayer.

For those who have gone before us and our hope for the future:
We remember those whose faithful acts shaped our lives;
Grant us courage to continue their legacy of love and justice.
God of simple acts, hear our prayer.

Pentecost 4 | Year C

God of all nations, we pray for the peoples of the world,
for those seeking justice, safety, and daily bread.
In the noise of violence, let peace be heard.
Hear our prayer, O God of love and justice.

We pray for Aotearoa and all who lead,
for wise decisions shaped by compassion and care.
May your reign of equity and courage be near.
Hear our prayer, O God of love and justice.

We pray for the church, your body in every place,
that we might live what we proclaim in prayer.
Teach us to forgive, to serve, and to speak boldly.
Hear our prayer, O God of love and justice.

For our neighbourhoods and communities,
where loneliness hides and needs go unseen,
may we bring connection, welcome, and healing.
Hear our prayer, O God of love and justice.

For all who suffer in body, mind, or spirit,
who cry out in silence, or who have lost the words,
give comfort through your Spirit and through us.
Hear our prayer, O God of love and justice.

And we remember those who have gone before us,
whose faith and witness light our path still.
Raise us too in hope to life beyond death.
Hear our prayer, O God of love and justice.

Pentecost 7 | Year C

For the peoples of the world,
where greed rules and violence persists,
for those seeking safety, peace, and dignity,
for places torn by war and inequality,
Clothe us in your grace, O Christ.

For our own nation, its leaders and decision-makers,
for justice to guide every law and policy,
for hearts that value the common good,
Clothe us in your grace, O Christ.

For your Church in every land and tradition,
for courage to shed what no longer serves love,
for a witness marked by truth and welcome,
Clothe us in your grace, O Christ.

For our local communities, where divisions run deep,
for neighbours in need of food, friendship, or hope,
for kindness to grow between strangers,
Clothe us in your grace, O Christ.

For all who suffer – in silence or in anguish,
for those grieving, those burdened by illness,
for healing, peace, and companionship,
Clothe us in your grace, O Christ.

For those who have gone before us in love,
for the promise of new life in Christ,
for our own faithful living in hope,
Clothe us in your grace, O Christ.

Pentecost 8 | Year C

We pray for the peoples of the world,
for justice to rise and mercy to rule,
for voices of peace to grow stronger than hate.
God of freedom, hear our prayer.

We pray for Aotearoa, for leaders and lawmakers,
that compassion would shape our policies,
and the last and least be uplifted.
God of freedom, hear our prayer.

We pray for your church in every place,
that we would follow Jesus with courage,
and choose people over rules, love over fear.
God of freedom, hear our prayer.

We pray for our neighbourhoods and communities,
that loneliness may be answered with welcome,
and kindness become our shared language.
God of freedom, hear our prayer.

We pray for those bent low by illness or grief,
those carrying burdens they cannot name,
that your healing spirit would restore and renew.
God of freedom, hear our prayer.

We remember those who have gone before us,
trusting in your promise of a new Jerusalem,
and give thanks for hope that cannot be shaken.
God of freedom, hear our prayer.

Pentecost 11 | Year C

For the peoples of the world –
where power exploits and dignity is denied,
where oceans rise and hopes recede,
may we honour each life and each shore with care.
God of the deep, stir our hearts to justice.

For our country and leaders –
that policy might protect both people and planet,
that courage may outweigh convenience,
and that wisdom may rise like a tide.
God of the deep, stir our hearts to justice.

For the church in all places –
may we stand with Onesimus and not with empire,
may our love be active and our theology embodied,
may we count the cost and still say yes.
God of the deep, stir our hearts to justice.

For our communities –
for neighbours displaced by storms and systems,
for sacred *va* between peoples and the land,
let connection grow where division once ruled.
God of the deep, stir our hearts to justice.

For the suffering –
those burdened by climate grief, illness, or silence,
those whose dignity is worn thin by injustice,
may healing rise like a tide of mercy.
God of the deep, stir our hearts to justice.

For the ancestors and saints –
those who left shorelines and legacies behind,
those who taught us to stand, to sing, to resist –
may we carry their light and live their love.
God of the deep, stir our hearts to justice.

Pentecost 13 | Year C

We pray now for ourselves and others:

For the peoples of the world,
where violence grows and injustice seems to win,
where envy corrodes and the powerful go unchecked,
may your quiet justice take root.
God, renew our trust in your unfolding way.

For our nation and leaders,
amidst growing pressure, fragile hope, and public weariness,
may policies reflect mercy, patience, and courage.
God, renew our trust in your unfolding way.

For the Church, global and local,
that we may serve without seeking status,
offering humble witness to your transforming love.
God, renew our trust in your unfolding way.

For our communities and neighbours,
where anxiety grows and people are stretched thin,
may small acts of kindness shift the story.
God, renew our trust in your unfolding way.

For all who suffer, in body, mind, or spirit,
those living with doubt, illness, grief, or despair –
may faith, even the size of a mustard seed, bring comfort.
God, renew our trust in your unfolding way.

For those who have gone before us,
whose faithful lives lit quiet fires of grace,
may we walk gently in their footsteps,
trusting the God who is still writing the story.
God, renew our trust in your unfolding way.

Pentecost 17 | Year C

50 – Offering and Blessing of Offering

God's grace surprises us again and again.
Let us respond with generosity and joy.
Your free will offering will now be received.

Blessing of Offering (said together)

Bless these gifts, O God of new beginnings.
May they feed your people and nourish your world.
Use them to build your kingdom of love.
In the name of Christ, who calls and sends us.

Easter 3 | Year C

As Tabitha used her hands for good,
so too we offer our gifts for the life of the world.
Your free will offering will now be received.

Blessing of Offering (said together)

Bless these gifts with the spirit of resurrection.
May they clothe the naked, comfort the grieving,
and lift the fallen.
Transform them into acts of justice and love.
In the name of Christ, our risen hope.

Easter 4 | Year C

When Jesus saw the man by the pool,
he offered healing before it was asked for.
Let us offer freely, trusting that our gifts
can be part of God's work of restoration.
Your free will offering will now be received.

Blessing of Offering (said together)

Bless these gifts and those who give them.
Let them be signs of compassion and hope.
Use them to lift up the weary and renew what is broken.
In your mercy, may all find strength to rise.

Easter 6 | Year C

God clothes us with grace beyond measure.
Let us respond with gifts of gratitude and hope.
Your free will offering will now be received.

Blessing of Offering (said together)

Bless these gifts, O Christ,
that they may weave healing in our world.
Bless the givers, that they may clothe others with love.
Bless our lives, that we may bear your image brightly.

Pentecost 2 | Year C

With grateful hearts, we bring our gifts and ourselves.
May our offerings become simple acts of love and healing.
Your free will offering will now be received.

Blessing of Offering (said together)

Bless these gifts and those who give them.
Use them to bring healing where there is hurt.
May they build peace and justice in every place.
And may they reflect your boundless grace.

Pentecost 4 | Year C

Just as Christ gave everything to raise us to new life,
we bring these gifts as signs of gratitude and hope.
Your free will offering will now be received.

Blessing of Offering (said together)

Bless these gifts and all who give.
Root our generosity in love, not obligation.
Use these offerings to build your reign of grace.
And grow in us a spirit of joyful trust.

Pentecost 7 | Year C

We give, not to build barns, but to build your kingdom.
We offer not surplus, but what matters most.
Your free will offering will now be received.

Blessing of Offering (said together)

Bless these gifts and those who give them.
May they be used to bring justice and joy.
Let this offering be a sign of our trust.
And may we always be rich toward you.

Pentecost 8 | Year C

Let us respond with grateful hearts
Let us offer what we have in joy
Your free will offering will now be received.

Blessing of Offering (said together)

With gratitude we bring our gifts
With awe we honour your Kingdom
With love we bless those in need
With trust we follow your Way.

Pentecost 11 | Year C

We do not give out of surplus
We give because we believe another way is possible
Your free will offering will now be received.

Blessing of Offering (said together)

Bless these gifts and those who offer them
Let them serve the voiceless and the vulnerable
Let our giving echo our discipleship
May our lives and gifts reflect your justice.

Pentecost 13 | Year C

Let us trust in the Lord and do good
Let us give not for gain, but for grace
Your free will offering will now be received.

Blessing of Offering (said together)

Bless these gifts and all who give them
Let them nourish quiet acts of justice
May our faith be lived through generosity
And our service reflect your love.

Pentecost 17 | Year C

51 – Benediction / Sending Forth

Go now, with eyes open to grace that surprises.
Let courage guide you, like Ananias stepping forward.
Let love restore you, like Peter beside the fire.
Share what you have seen and heard.
Feed others, bless strangers, follow Christ.
And may the Spirit give you strength for the journey.

Easter 3 | Year C

Go now, as those who are known by the Shepherd.
Walk with faith that listens, and love that acts.
Let no fear pull you from the grasp of grace.
May the voice of Christ echo in your heart.
May you be led in peace, renewed in compassion,
And held forever in the unity of God's love.

Easter 4 | Year C

Go now, as Paul went, guided by vision and Spirit.
Go as Lydia did, with open heart and open hands.
May your home become a place of welcome and witness.
May your life reflect courage, faith, and generosity.
Christ goes before you; the Spirit empowers you.
Walk in grace, and live in peace.

Easter 6 | Year C

Go now, clothed in Christ's mercy and strength.
Cross every boundary for the sake of love.
Tell your story of healing and hope.
See no stranger, call no one "other."
Let compassion be your garment and peace your path.
The Spirit goes with you, weaving new life.

Pentecost 2 | Year C

Go now, with humility that welcomes wisdom,
With courage that embraces simple tasks.
Be agents of peace where fear divides,
And vessels of healing where pain endures.
Trust that the Spirit goes before and within you,
Sending you out in love and resilient hope.

Pentecost 4 | Year C

Go now in the strength of persistent prayer.
Let your life be shaped by grace and trust.
Seek God in the daily and the difficult.
Forgive as you are forgiven.
Give as you have received.
And walk always in the Way of Christ.

Pentecost 7 | Year C

Go now and set your heart on things above.
Clothe yourselves in mercy, kindness, and courage.
Do not hoard your gifts – share them with the world.
Let go of fear and walk in freedom.
Christ is your life, hidden and revealed.
And God goes with you, now and always.

Pentecost 8 | Year C

Go now, standing tall in God's grace
Walk freely in the Way of compassion
Let nothing shake your hope or silence your praise
For you are part of a Kingdom that endures
Go with reverence, go with joy, go with courage
In the name of the Living Christ.

Pentecost 11 | Year C

Go now with the courage to love where it costs
Go now with the clarity to name what must change
Go now to enter the *va* with all creation
Go now, reordered and renewed by Christ
Go with the deep peace of the Spirit beneath you
And with hope rising, like the tide.

Pentecost13 | Year C

Go now with mustard seed faith
Live not for applause but from abundance
Let your trust be deeper than your doubt
And your service be quiet, steady, and free
May delight, not duty, guide your walk
And may you go in peace, held always by grace.

Pentecost 17 | Year C

52 – Children's Talk & Introducing the Theme Suggestions

God's Call Reversed

(Moments of Wonder or Surprise, Analogies and Metaphors, Visuals and Props)

Show a large card with the word "NO" on it. After some discussion about saying no to God, flip the card upside down to reveal the word "ON" or "GO". Talk about how Saul said "no" to Jesus at first – but that didn't stop Jesus from turning his life *on*. Invite children to consider how God might be turning them "on" to something new.

Transformation Glasses

(Visuals and Props, Interactive Participation, Analogies and Metaphors)

Hand out coloured cellophane "lenses" or decorated cardboard glasses. Ask: If these let you see the world the way God sees it, what would be different? Talk about how Saul started seeing people with love instead of fear, and how we can see others the same way. Link to transformation and renewed perspective.

Who Are You Listening To?

(Interactive Participation, Analogies and Metaphors, Dramatisation)

Play a simple "follow the voice" game with one blindfolded child guided by voices – some giving wrong directions, one giving the right one. Talk about how Saul had to stop listening to angry voices and start hearing Jesus. Reflect together: How do we know which voice is God's? How can we listen better?

Easter 3 | Year C

The Shepherd's Call

Use toy sheep scattered around the church and hide them behind chairs or furniture. Speak in different silly voices before using your normal "shepherd voice" to call them back. Let children decide which voice to follow. Discuss how Jesus says we can learn to recognise his voice when we listen carefully. Relate this to John 10 and how we are always held in God's care. End with a joyful "baa choir" of sheep voices!

Good Shepherd Selfie

Bring a mirror or selfie frame. Invite each child to come up and look into the mirror while you say, "You are one of Jesus' sheep. He knows your name." Then ask, "What do you think Jesus sees when he looks at you?" Link this to belonging and being held in God's love. This moment combines wonder, reflection, and joyful affirmation. Take a group photo if appropriate!

Heartbeats of Faith

Have the children each find their pulse on their wrist or neck. Sit in quiet for a moment and feel it. Say: "Every heartbeat reminds us we are alive – and that we can use this life to do good." Link back to Tabitha's restored life and how we can use our life well. Let children wonder aloud what they'd like to be known for.

Easter 4 | Year C

Getting Stuck

(Analogy)

Bring a backpack or small suitcase filled with heavy objects. Talk about how we sometimes carry heavy things (worries, sadness, doubt) that stop us from moving. Then lighten the load by unpacking the backpack or suitcase and explain how Jesus helps us rise again and move forward.

Get Up and Grow

(Metaphor)

Bring a wilting plant and water it. Talk about how plants need care to grow – like the man at the pool needed someone to believe in him. Ask: Who helps you grow strong and hopeful when you feel down?

The Heart That Opens

(Moments of Wonder)

Hold a heart-shaped box and open it slowly. Inside, place something glowing or beautiful. Say: "Lydia's heart was opened by God – just like this." Invite children to think about what it means to open their hearts to kindness and love.

Easter 6 | Year C

Chains and Freedom

(Interactive + Visual)

Use a rope to bind one volunteer gently (hands or arms). Ask how it feels to be restricted. Then "set them free" while saying: "Jesus sets us free from what holds us back – fear, shame, feeling left out. And we're all included in God's love."

Build a Wall, Then Break It Down

(Interactive + Mission Link)

Stack cardboard boxes as a barrier between the groups of children (e.g. 'boys vs. girls', 'young vs. old', 'rich vs. poor'). Knock it down dramatically, then say: "Paul says there's no more 'us' and 'them' – we are one!"

The Welcome Circle

(Participation + Inclusion)

Form a circle. Invite others in: "What if someone was different from us – do they belong?" Let children invite imaginary or real people into the circle. Conclude: "Jesus welcomes everyone. And so do we."

Pentecost 2 | Year C

Act out the Naaman story

(Dramatisation and Role-Playing)

Invite a few children to act out Naaman, the servant girl, Elisha's messenger, and the wise servants. Highlight how small, humble voices and simple acts can lead to big changes.

Small acts of kindness

(Reflection and Response)

Ask the children to think about someone they can help this week with a small act of kindness. Provide small paper hearts for them to write their ideas on and place them at the foot of the communion table or cross.

Spreading Peace

(Dramatisation and Role-Playing)

Have children pretend to visit different houses (chairs or sections of the church) offering peace and asking to help, just as the seventy-two disciples did.

Pentecost 4 | Year C

Prayer Puzzle

(Interactive Participation)

Give each child a card with one line of the Lord's Prayer (Luke's version). Work together to place them in order. Talk about what each line means in simple language.

My Prayer Pebble

(Reflection and Response)

Give each child a small stone to hold during a quiet moment. Invite them to silently thank God or ask for help. This tactile moment introduces the practice of prayer.

Prayer Tree

(Reflection and Response)

Create a simple "tree" on a wall or board. Children can write or draw their prayers on leaf-shaped paper and add them to the tree as a growing act of faith and hope.

Pentecost 7 | Year C

Old Shirt, New Shirt

(Visual & Analogy)

Bring in an old, ripped shirt and a beautiful, clean new one. Ask, "Which one would you rather wear?" Explain that Paul says following Jesus means taking off the "old" (anger, lies, greed) and putting on something new (kindness, love). Let the children hold and compare them.

Bigger Barns Game

(Interactive & Role-Play)

Give each child paper cut-outs of 'crops' (grain, fruit). Ask them to collect as many as possible – but then reveal they can't take them home! Then talk about the parable: What really matters is not how much we keep, but how we share.

Community Weaving

(Mission & Participation)

Have children weave a simple cord or ribbon together, each one adding a strand. Talk about how Paul says we are one in Christ – no matter our background. God makes a new community out of many different people.

Pentecost 8 | Year C

Stack of heavy books in a backpack

(Prop)

Show a child trying to wear a backpack filled with books, representing burdens. Remove each book labelled with things like "fear", "rules", "loneliness", until they can stand tall. Ask: "What helped her stand up straight again in today's story?"

Rules vs. Love traffic lights

(Metaphor)

Create two traffic light signs – one says "STOP, RULES FIRST!" and the other "GO, LOVE FIRST!". Use simple scenarios (e.g. helping a friend, sharing lunch) to ask: "Which one would Jesus choose?"

Who needs help standing up today?

(Link to Mission)

Ask: "Who in our world today is bent low – by sadness, hunger, unfairness?" Then brainstorm ways we can be like Jesus and help others stand tall. Invite a mission partner or story from your church's outreach to be shared.

Pentecost 11 | Year C

The Layered Jar Experiment

Show a clear jar with layers of sand, water, and oil. Ask, "What's at the bottom?" "What's in between?" Let the layers settle. Talk about how like this jar, our world and our lives have layers – some beautiful, some painful – and Jesus invites us to look below the surface, just like Paul did with Onesimus. A reflective moment can follow where everyone watches in silence.

Message in a Bottle: God's Call to Us

Prepare scrolls with short messages like "Set others free," "Care for creation," "See people as God does," "Take up your cross." Put them in plastic bottles (e.g. like small peanut butter jars with screw top lids) and let children come up to open and read them. After each, ask: "What might that look like today?" A powerful visual and discussion starter about receiving and responding to God's deeper message.

"Ocean of Connections" Web Activity

Using a ball of blue yarn, form a web by tossing it between children and adults, with each person saying a way we're connected (e.g. "I care about dolphins," "I love my brother," "I use water every day"). As the web forms, talk about V*a* – the sacred space between us – and how discipleship means honouring those ties, not tearing them apart.

Pentecost 13 | Year C | Ocean Sunday

The Mustard Seed Challenge

(Visuals, Movement, Wonder)

Hold up a tiny mustard seed and a large object (e.g. a plant or tree photo) and ask, "Can something this small really move something this big?" Hand out small mustard seeds in envelopes for each child or family to take home. Invite them to plant the seed or tape it somewhere visible to remind them that even small faith can grow and do great things.

Unseen Heroes Drama

(Role-Play, Surprise, Reflection)

Set up a quick skit: one person does flashy tasks and looks for praise, while another does simple background jobs quietly. Ask the children: Who did more to help? Talk about how Jesus notices every act of service – even when no one else does. Thank the "quiet helpers" in your congregation.

Stillness is Powerful

(Quiet Reflection, Movement, Wonder)

Guide the group into a moment of stillness. Light a candle. Ask everyone to close their eyes, breathe deeply, and "wait patiently before the Lord." After 30 seconds, invite them to open their eyes and share what they noticed. Highlight how hard stillness can be – but also how powerful it is to listen for God.

Pentecost 17 | Year C

Links to Websites and Resources

I have compiled into one PDF document all the links to websites and other digital resources referred to in this book.

After downloading the PDF, you can click the links within it to access the websites and resources.

Purchasers of this book can download the **Links PDF** here:

https://tinyurl.com/2mk9357h

Worship Resources and Books by Philip Garside

Visit: philipgarsidebooks.com

Worship at Hand

Your ready-to-use resource designed especially for ministers, lay preachers, and worship leaders who want to offer thoughtful, inclusive services without the last-minute scramble.

Each week's material includes:

- A well-structured, Revised Common Lectionary-based Order of Service

- A 1000-1200 word sermon

- 10 ideas for the Children's Talk

- 12 hymn suggestions exclusively from *Alleluia Aotearoa, Faith Forever Singing, and Hope Is Our Song*

- A royalty-free image to use in your service visuals and Order of Service.

Annual Subscription, Monthly and Weekly purchase options available.

Worship Outside the Box

A weekly blog of Creative Ideas for Leading Worship

Something new for ministers, lay preachers, and worship leaders to try each week.

You can also listen to an audio narration of each post.

Short Reflections

A free 250-word reflection on the one or two of the Revised Common Lectionary readings for the week.

Based on the content of the *Worship at Hand* sermon.

Let Your Light Shine Through

62 Fresh Sermons to Inspire Your Preaching (2nd Edition)

A dynamic collection of 62 creative sermons designed to inspire new and experienced preachers, deepen theological understanding, and engage congregations.

Available in print and eBook formats.

Kindle A Flame

Songs, Prayers & Poems (Creative Worship Volume 1)

Inspiring songs, prayers, and poems to uplift and energise worship, fostering creative and heartfelt spiritual expression.

PDF eBook.

www.ingramcontent.com/pod-product-compliance
Lightning Source LLC
Chambersburg PA
CBHW020409150626
46554CB00012B/425